T0113929

Shattered

Is God Really Using
Our Broken Pieces

Bryan Dixon

WestBow
PRESS®
A DIVISION OF THOMAS NELSON
& ZONDERVAN

WestBow Press books may be ordered through booksellers or by contacting:

WestBow Press
A Division of Thomas Nelson & Zondervan
1663 Liberty Drive
Bloomington, IN 47403
www.westbowpress.com
844-714-3454

ISBN: 978-1-6642-4578-5 (sc)
ISBN: 978-1-6642-4577-8 (e)

Print information available on the last page.

WestBow Press rev. date: 10/05/2021

Dedication

To my wife Eileen, that season of life that left us feeling completely shattered was one of the hardest one's I have experienced so far. But I am so thankful to God that He brought our family through it and that I had you by my side every step of the way. I love you, forever!

To my mom and dad, thank you for your unconditional love and unrelenting support of me throughout my entire life. I appreciate the endless sacrifices that you have made on behalf of me and continue to make on behalf of our family and your grandchildren. I know that COVID-19 has the timeline of us seeing each other again, unknown. But I am sincerely looking forward to that day. I love you two with all of my heart!

Finally, I especially want to dedicate this book to our "Juneteenth" Group and Fannie and her family. Thank you all for walking alongside of our family during the season of life that we felt completely shattered.

God Prepares Us for The Storm of Brokenness

It was mile marker 13, on US Highway 163 in southern Utah's Monument Valley. I found myself walking down this long road in what seemed to be a strange but telling dream one spring night as I slept restlessly at my home in Reading, Pennsylvania. I still find it a bit humorous, because for those of you who may not recognize this location, it is the Forrest Gump road. The point in the movie Forrest Gump where Forrest stopped running. I suppose this was meaningful for me since Forrest Gump was one of my favorite movies as a child.

Anyway, back to my dream; as I am making my way down this seemingly never-ending road between the Grand Canyon and Moab (Arches National Park), I see dark rain clouds rolling in, hear the sound of thunder crashing and see lightning at a distance. I am not scared, but I am anxious because I know a rainstorm is coming as there are no blue skies in sight, and I am all alone. I continue walking, convincing myself that *it is what it is,* and I'll be fine, I am about to be poured on but at some point, I'll be out of it.

Suddenly, I feel this heavy presence next to me, completely invisible except for its monstrous hand reaching out and grabbing mine. Immediately, a sense of peace and comfort came over me; I mean, I still knew that there was no way of avoiding the storm, but even though I couldn't see this thing with the monstrous hand, I knew that even though I was alone, I wasn't really alone.

Still sleeping restlessly my dream takes me to a different location. It's like I am on a movie set seeing different scenes, but I am the main actor. I do, however, recognize this new location in my dream, or on set if you will. It is not one off of any movies that I had ever seen, but rather my former home on a missionary base that I used to live on in Haiti. There is a gentleman there with me, we are not conversing much at all, but oddly enough this man is cleaning everything out of my refrigerator. Finally, my alarm clock goes off and it's time for me to get ready for work.

On my drive into work I knew that this dream had significance, and I was afraid to acknowledge just what it might mean. There was absolutely no doubt in my mind that this dream came to me directly from God. As a matter of fact, I knew deep in my heart that the invisible thing that reached out its monstrous hand and grabbed mine in the dream, was the Holy Spirit. I had never had an encounter with God like this before and although I knew that this was exactly what that was, I was just trying to either over analyze it or brush it off as just another dream like any other night.

All day as I was hard at work on the busy construction site that we were on, I could not get this dream out of my mind. I truly believe that God was gracious enough to number one, allow me to recognize that it came from Him and that He still speaks to people in any and every way, too including visions and dreams. Encounters like this with God weren't just reserved for the great men and women that I had read and learned about from the Bible. Secondly, looking back now, I can see His kindness in equipping me with the ability to perceive what He was speaking to me through the dream. But my pride and human reasoning kept trying to convince myself that I was way overthinking this, that I did not actually hear from God.

However, the more I wrestled with the significance of this dream throughout my day, I was able to recall a song that came to me soon after the COVID-19 lockdown began just a month or so prior.

We have an anchor that keeps the soul, steadfast and sure while the billows roll, fastened to a rock which cannot move, grounded firm and deep in the savior's love (Priscilla Owens, We Have an Anchor).

In case you can't tell by those song lyrics, I was raised in a pretty traditional church setting and have grown to thoroughly enjoy hymns. Soon after the lockdown began in 2020, I took a video of myself singing this song and posted it on a family Facebook page jokingly suggesting that my fear of Corona Virus reminded me that we have an anchor. On this day though, I was able to make a distinct connection with the song that I decided to randomly sing one morning *(because I do find joy in singing randomly)* and the dream that I had just the night before. I was walking down the never-ending Forrest Gump road, the billowing clouds were rolling preparing for a massive storm, and I was alone until I wasn't alone and my anchor, the Holy Spirit came and took my hand to keep me grounded and firm as we prepared to go through the storm. Wow, I am an absolute spiritual genius, I just paralleled a song that came to me with a dream that God gave me and interpreted it perfectly. I might just be as good as Joseph or one of the other great prophets of the Bible. Yeah Right!

At this point I feel like I am not only completely over analyzing the dream that I had, but I thought to myself that I must be thinking in a blasphemous way and acting like one of those over spiritual religious people. Nonetheless, the significance of this dream was weighing heavy on me and I had to tell someone about it. Not just what the dream was and its unique parallel with one of my favorite hymns, but also its significance for me personally. Obviously, the only person there was to tell that I knew would listen and take me completely seriously was my wife. And for the record, considering the fact that we are married and one flesh, I knew that this dream had significance for her too as well as our five children.

So, that evening as we were getting cleaned up after dinner and the children were in bed, I gave her the whole rundown. I tell her about my journey down Forrest Gump road, to which she stared at me completely confused, and I determined right then that she had to get with the times and watch this classic movie. I thought I'd give her a pass though since she's not American, but strongly suggested that watching the movie would give her a greater glimpse into American culture and history. I am sure that could be debated. She then told me that she knows what the movie Forrest Gump is because it was also her favorite childhood movie, she was just confused by me referring to a road that I was walking down as Forrest Gump road. Needless to say, I was relieved knowing that she watched this great American classic. Anyway, I told her that I sincerely felt that I was walking with the Holy Spirit down this road in my dream and that a major storm was about to take over, but I was going to be okay because I wasn't alone, even though I was. I then told her about the man that was taking food out of my refrigerator at my old home in Haiti. Knowing my wife, I am sure in her mind she thought, "yeah, I knew my husband was weird and eccentric sometimes, but this kind of makes it official." By the way, in no way do I believe that these thoughts would come to her because she does not believe that the Lord still speaks to people in supernatural ways, but because she would be right in the fact that my personality tends to be weird and eccentric at times! Thankfully, however, those weren't the words that came out of her mouth. Instead, she so graciously asked, what do you think it means.

I took a deep breath and rested my hand on top of hers as it was lying on the kitchen counter. "I believe that God is about to walk with me through a long, hard, dark and lonely season of life. I've been through these before, but could always push through on my own strength, even though in reality it was always God's. However, I believe the presence of the Holy Spirit and His monstrous hand reaching out to me on the Forrest Gump road was a reassurance and promise that He will be with me through it because there is no chance at all that I'll be able to get through the upcoming season of life on my own strength. In fact, trying to use any of my strength at all would only end up in complete chaos and defeat. As far as the man taking food out of my refrigerator in Haiti, I have no clue who the man was, it's not how I ever pictured Jesus, but maybe it was Him, or maybe an Angel, or maybe just some random guy, I am not sure. But I believe that the significance of that part of my dream is that God is going to not only continue to remove the unclean things out of my heart and my life, but also, simply remove the old things that have been with me for a long time, or even a lifetime. Kind of like when we go grocery shopping you know, and some things end up staying in the fridge for a very long time. Eventually, they either go bad and become unclean or unhealthy to eat and we get rid of it, or we just realize that it may not have an expiration date, but it's time to get something new. I needed to tell you because although I don't have any idea what this season is going to look like for me, I know that this is going to impact our entire family, and so we have to pray hard and be prepared."

My wife just looked at me with tears in her eyes. I asked her if she thought I was being dramatic and seeing into something that wasn't there. But my lovely wife just looked at me and said; "no, I don't think you're being dramatic, and I trust and hope that whatever this upcoming season, looks like for us that God will use it to bring us two a lot closer as well. We just have to stay strong in our faith and completely trust God through it all."

Admittedly, although we both knew that this dream and its significance truly did come from God, when my wife made the comment about staying strong in our faith, for the first time in my life it really did scare me. Trust God through hard times and have faith that can move mountains; I realized right at that moment that these two religious catch phrases, that indeed are biblical, had never truly been put to the test in my life. I sincerely felt this, because a strong fear honestly came over me as my wife and I discussed this and began praying about it.

Recently, I read the book *Dangerous Prayers* by Craig Groeschel. It changed my entire outlook on prayer and showed me how shallow my prayer life had truly been throughout my life as a Christian. In the book, Groeschel challenges his Christian readers and audience to rid ourselves of ineffective, lukewarm faith-like prayers. Instead, he suggests replacing them with raw and dangerous prayers that just might result in loss, rejection, failure, and fear of the unknown as gateways of welcoming the blessings of God. Honestly, after reading the book, I was quite afraid to pray and didn't for a few days.

At the same time though, I reflected back on the season of my life that occurred, and that I am technically still in (I think), after my dream of walking down Forrest Gump road alone with the Holy Spirit. I was able to recall two distinct times that I accidently prayed a dangerous prayer and all of the miniature dangerous prayers that I prayed during that season in desperation, anger, and confusion.

In January of 2020, like every good person bringing in the new year, I did the Christian thing and prayed to God with gratitude for a great 2019 and asked His blessing on 2020. But there was one aspect of this prayer that was truly different and came from a very sincere part of my heart. I asked God to please speak to me supernaturally as a way of revealing and uncovering the true calling that He had for my life. I must have been feeling pretty bold, because I remember adding that I don't care what it is, I just want to know as soon as possible because there had to be more to life than just going through the motions. Well, a few months later came the dream of me walking down Forrest Gump road. I know, many people would consider this complete coincidence or even my over analyzing and over spiritualizing something that wasn't there. But when I put all of the pieces together there is no doubt in my mind that the encounter, I had that spring night in my dream was God answering my prayer of Him speaking to me supernaturally.

The second distinct time I remember praying a dangerous prayer was the night after the dream when I told my wife what my interpretation of the dream was. Knowing that I had her full support, we both prayed together and trusted that this supernatural encounter indeed was from God, together we continued and prayed the simple yet dangerous prayer, God whatever you're going to walk with us through, we're willing and ready.

Having received a fresh perspective on the true impact

and power of prayer after reading Groeschel's *Dangerous Prayers*, I realize now how absolutely insane we were for praying this. Furthermore, whenever the sting of the pain that the next season of life would bring us resurfaces, even now as I write, my human reasoning and flesh wishes we would have prayed something like; *God, I don't think we have the emotional or mental capacity to go through whatever you have in mind. We have five children under five years old, one of whom is a newborn and two that we're about to adopt through foster care. We don't have any grandparents that live close by, and our friend circle is a bit small too. Not because we're not likeable, I don't think so anyway, but simply because we're all in different seasons of life. It's hard enough that both of our main support systems live many miles away and we're trying our best here to take care of our children, pay the bills, and of course grow as a married couple. So, although not near as intense as what you called your only begotten son to do, I want to end this prayer the way He ended His in the garden of Gethsemane and ask you to please take this cup away from us* (Matthew 26: 36-46, NIV).

Of course, we'd be leaving out the most selfless part of Jesus's prayer in the garden, *yet not my will but yours (Matthew 26:42, NIV).* Because my wife and I both have a true heart's desire to serve and honor God by fulfilling the assignment that He has ordained us for on this earth, I will forever be grateful that we did not pray that prayer and instead prayed the simple yet accidental dangerous one, whatever you're going to walk with us through, we're willing and ready.

One thing that I learned through it all, from the accidental dangerous prayers, to them being answered in

God's way and timing, to them being fulfilled in God's way and timing, is the truth that the Prophet Isaiah spoke. *"For my thoughts are not your thoughts, neither are your ways my ways," declares the Lord. "As the heavens are higher than the earth, so are my ways higher than your ways and my thoughts than your thoughts"* (Isaiah 55:8-9, NIV).

When I prayed my original dangerous prayer asking God to speak to me in a supernatural way, if I am honest, I had my own agenda and ideas for how I wanted it answered. I mean I had read in the Bible about all the miraculous ways that God spoke to people and lead them into the extraordinary callings that He had for them. He sent a prophet to dub David the future King of Israel, and He even sent an Angel to tell Samson's mother, who had a barren womb at the time, that she was going to give birth to a son who would be used to deliver Israel out of the hand of the Philistines. He spoke through dreams to Joseph who would eventually become the ruler of Egypt, and of course sent His only begotten son who not only died for the sins of the world but took a group of twelve unpredictable average guys and radically changed the world. Eleven of them even went on to lead great ministries and ten were martyred for their faith. Why was I any different, I even told God that I no longer wanted to just go through the motions of life, I was ready to embark on this extraordinary calling that he must have for my life

As I reflect on my journey from the day that I prayed dangerously asking God for a supernatural sign, to where I am at today, I cannot help but to consider one of Jesus's critical lessons in a few of His parables throughout the Gospels. Jesus proclaims a few times, *but many who are first will be last, and many who are last will be first* (Matthew 19:30, NIV). Furthermore, if I am honest with myself about the subtle selfishness that was behind this dangerous prayer, I am reminded of what God told the prophet Samuel when He sent him to anoint David as the King of Israel. *But the Lord said to Samuel, "Do not consider his appearance or his height, for I have rejected him. The Lord does not look at the things people look at. People look at the outward appearance, but the Lord looks at the heart* (1 Samuel 16:7, NIV).

I am incredibly grateful to God for His graciousness and mercy and willingness to still answer prayers, even when there is selfish ambition behind them. This bold prayer requesting a supernatural encounter with God as a way of gaining keen insight into the massive calling that God must surely be leading me into, completely put me and my desires at the focal point rather than God. I mean I was even arrogant enough to compare myself to some of the great people that God used in the Bible, suggesting that I was just as worthy to be used by God in a way that I would be remembered forever. Even in my longing to pursue and live the life that God wanted me to, I fell trap to wanting to be first in the world's eyes, and justified it by showing honor for and desiring to be like the ancient hero's that God used, completely based of off their outward successes.

David got to lead a nation and was known for being a man after God's own heart. But when I read through the Psalms it is pretty clear that the journey there was dangerously difficult resulting in many dark times of depression and real near-death experiences. These aren't just fictional stories to make it sound good, David actually went through all of that brokenness to get there. God used Samson to fulfill the purpose that He wanted, but even through it all Samson abused the gifts that God provided him with to the point that he became vulnerable in relinquishing His God given strength. He then reaped harshly the consequences of the sin that he sowed, even until death when he cried out to the Lord one last time in shear brokenness.

Joseph got to encounter God through dreams of what was to come in his life, only for it to result in family betrayal, becoming a slave, and imprisonment. He endured many years of heartache and turmoil until he eventually became ruler, and when the dreams that God gave him representing his brothers bowing down to him came to pass, the assignment was to serve them food in their time of need, and to forgive them in that moment. It was many years of brokenness before Joseph's assignment came to pass, and to reiterate, although the gift that God gave to him of interpreting dreams lead to him obtaining a position as ruler, this was not his assignment. His assignment was to serve and forgive his brothers, despite the years of brokenness that they caused him.

Then God sent Jesus, His only begotten son. God in the flesh came and dwelt among us here on earth to fulfill an assignment. *For the son of man came to seek and to save the lost* (Luke 19:10, NIV), and the way in which He was going to fulfill His mission was *to serve and not be served, and to give his life as a ransom for many* (Matthew 20:28, NIV). He too discipled others to do the same, but the only way they would truly be equipped to live out this mission and purpose, would be to give up everything to follow Him and His commands. Only through shear brokenness and sacrifice until the end did eleven of Jesus's twelve core disciples fulfill their assignment. Jesus Christ, the Son of God himself, had the ultimate assignment of being completely broken on the cross for the sins of the world.

Wow! All of these biblical greats, too including God himself, and the only common theme I see in all of their mission's is brokenness. Each one experienced betrayal, fear, depression, weeping, and even the desire to abort their mission. All of the biblical greats, even the one's not mentioned here, realized and experienced the truth; that the only way for their assignment to come to pass was for life as they knew it to become completely shattered.

Shattered is such a strong and intense word, but I believe that it truly captures the expectation that God has for us when the timing comes for us to fulfill our assignment. The definition(s) of shattered are *to break or cause to break suddenly and violently into pieces; to damage or destroy; or to upset greatly* (Oxford Dictionary). In realizing that this is a prerequisite to fulfilling our God given assignment here on earth, while also recognizing that the most impactful assignment ever given was Jesus's death on the cross, I can see a glimpse into what God meant when He spoke through the prophet Isaiah reminding us that *his thoughts are not our thoughts, neither are his ways our ways* (Isaiah 55:8, NIV).

Clearly God's way of thinking and approach to doing things do not even remotely reflect our human finite hearts and minds, and definitely are not according to the world's standards. Society and culture will tell us that in order to achieve greatness we must focus on our strengths and maintain a positive mindset. Although we'll absolutely go through hard times and difficulties, we need to grin, bear it, and press on; not dwelling on our weaknesses or trials because *no one cares*. But Paul claims, *for Christ's sake, I delight in weaknesses, in insults, in hardships, in persecutions, in difficulties. For when I am weak, then I am strong* (2 Corinthians 12:9-11, NIV). Jesus comforts us by proclaiming, *come to me, all who are weary and burdened, and I will give you rest. Take my yoke upon you and learn from me, for I am gentle and humble in heart, and you will find rest for your souls. For my yoke is easy and my burden is light* (Matthew 11: 28-30, NIV). So, while the world teaches toughness, independence, and that no one cares on your path to greatness; God promises the exact opposite, that He is gentle, tender hearted, and cares so much that He invites us to put our weariness and burdens upon Him.

Furthermore, culture and society's idea of greatness is absolutely not God's idea of greatness. In teaching His disciples Jesus said, *you know that the rulers of the Gentiles lord it over them, and their high officials exercise authority over them. Not so with you. Instead, whoever wants to be great among you must be your servant and whoever wants to be first must be your slave* (Matthew 20: 25-27, NIV). So, according to Jesus, if you want to be great, you must become the lowest of the low. Looks like I got that wrong too so far considering the fact that I have a master's degree in Ministry with a Leadership Studies concentration, definitely not a servanthood focus. Well, I guess I have taken a number of servant leadership classes throughout my time in University. Seriously though, it's not about the degree, and clearly I am not opposed to higher education as a way of pursuing your God given assignment for your time here on earth, but for myself, I am realizing that while my heart's desire for a long time has been to serve God and fulfill my assignment, I have been actively pursuing it with the world's strategies and standards in mind, and not the Lord's. I suppose this is why I've found myself often chasing after new things, because the world says to keep going after bigger and better. Don't get me wrong, I also firmly believe that Christians often misuse or misinterpret what it means to be content. While some Christians may not be going after bigger and better like society teaches us, some of these same Christians remain stagnant and their idea of contentment keeps them from ever even coming close to completing their God given assignment.

However, many of us do have a pure heart's desire to fulfill the assignment that God has put us on earth to accomplish for His Kingdom and His Glory. For His Kingdom and for His Glory, words that I've always uttered but was never sincere in my heart about. I know God called and lead people into radical life changing assignments, and that has always been something I longed for deeply. But I wanted to be the one to take the glory and credit for it, and the radical life changing assignment had to of course measure up to society's standards. Don't get me wrong, I have always been moved by the Bible stories like the one about the women who poured perfume on Jesus's head and feet and when she was rebuked for it Jesus said, *she has done a beautiful thing to me…where ever the Gospel is preached throughout the world, what she has done will always be told, in memory of her* (Matthew 26:10;13, NIV). But I preferred my story to be more like King David's or even his son King Solomon, known for honor and riches. And, this could happen if I was careful to embark on my assignment in accordance with the standards of culture and society. I had to grind, be tough and keep myself together if things fell apart, become a great leader, and become first.

Thankfully, however, although I had my own strategy laid out for it and just needed God to show me what it was when I prayed for a supernatural message of my assignment, God showed me His way. He revealed to me that all I needed to know right than is that it starts with utter brokenness. The first step to even coming remotely close to stepping into the assignment that He has given me, is that I had to be broken to the point of no return. I had to be internally wrecked at my heart's core to the point that the only two options left would be to pursue God with everything I had, or willingly and even proudly walk away convinced that I can do this life on my own. I had to be shattered!

Knowing this, I was, and I am still completely terrified of what God's idea of brokenness and becoming completely shattered is. I have learned through it all, so far, that the religious teaching that God does not allow trials in your life to overwhelm you to the point that you cannot handle or bear it, is not true at all. As a matter of fact, this teaching is not even biblical in nature. I was reminded of this when reading Lysa Terkeurst's, *It's Not Supposed to be This Way.* My wife suggested that I read it because of the hard season that we were in together. She quotes what the actual verse says that we often misquote, take out of context, and likely lead people astray with when they find themselves in situations that are more than they can handle after promising them that God would never do this to them. Paul claims, *no temptation has overtaken you except what is common to mankind. And God is faithful;* **he will not let you be tempted beyond what you can bear.** *But when you are tempted, he will also provide a way out so that you can endure it* (1 Corinthians 10:13, NIV).

So, perhaps a better message for Christians to proclaim is that in the midst of the trials that you may be going through that are indeed beyond what you can bear, although the enemy will be hard at work tempting you, God will not allow the temptations to be beyond what you can bear. But the trials themselves, if you're serious about following God according the His standards and the standards that Christ exemplified, you can absolutely count on going through trials that are beyond what you can bear. It was this trying season that the Lord showed me He was prepared to walk with me and my family through.

The Brokenness is Personal

The arrogance and insensitivity of people within culture and societies today will have us convinced that because our situation could always be worse, you don't have the right to hurt from it. Or, with complete lack of compassion, empathy, or sympathy; we pour gas on the fire of the pain that others are feeling by reminding them that there is always someone else dealing with a greater hardship then they are. We even do this to ourselves a lot of times, don't we? I remember talking to a cousin of mine on social media, who I still have yet to meet, and we were just giving each other a little history of our lives and some of the things that we experienced. As she was explaining to me some of the dark times of her childhood I sincerely felt for her pain, but all I could respond with was, "I'm sorry you had to go through all of that." I'll never forget her response, as though she felt bad for hurting; "oh thanks, it's fine, it's life right, I always keep in mind that someone somewhere has it worse." Thankfully, because I know the pain of past trauma too well, as well having been deceived myself into thinking that the experiences in my life that hurt me were invalidated because other's experiences hurt them worse, I trust that I responded appropriately and with sensitivity. I simply told her, "that is true, but it doesn't take away from the pain that you had to deal with."

Manipulating people into believing that their pain doesn't really hurt them because someone else's pain hurts them more, is one of the worse things that we can do as Christians. The psalmist wrote, *the Lord is close to the brokenhearted and saves those who are crushed in spirit* (Psalm 34:18, NIV). Nowhere in that verse are there any contingencies or stipulations. Therefore, the Lord is just as close to and sensitive with someone who is sincerely heart broken and crushed spiritually as a result of losing a job and fears economic instability, as He is with the mourning widow or widower who may have also even just recently lost a child. I know, according to the world's standards, this isn't even a comparison. But God's ways are higher, and He is sensitive and comforting to us even in our personal brokenness, no matter how much the people around us remind us that our situation is nothing to be spiritually broken over.

The person without the Spirit does not accept the things that come from the Spirit of God but considers them foolishness and cannot understand them because they are discerned only through the Spirit (1 Corinthians 2:14, NIV). Perhaps the reason we as Christians so often misquote 1 Corinthians

10:13 and in doing so give others a false representation of God's role in our trials, is because we have become so deceived by the world's standards on how to handle and control our brokenness and in doing so became deaf to what the Spirit of God actually says. Jesus even had to remind Simon Peter of this when Peter's pride caused him to try and rebuke Jesus from fulfilling the assignment that his Father sent him here to do. *Jesus turned and said to Peter, "Get behind me, Satan! You are a stumbling block to me,* **you do not have in mind the concerns of God, but merely human concerns** (Matthew 16:23, NIV). Well, in looking at and analyzing these few Scripture references, I am a bit intrigued. It is almost as though we actually have to be in the right place Spiritually in order to be broken effectively.

So, it is imperative that I get myself at a solid place spiritually, that way I can reap the benefit of being broken, effectively? That has got to be the worse exchange ever in the history of things ever exchanged! In other words, that seems like a pretty awful deal to me! But seriously, we have got to be grounded and know who and where we are going to run to when everything turns into chaos and we become shattered. Because if we do not, it's not that we won't be able to get through it, although sometimes this is the case, but it's the fact that the only thing we'll reap from that brokenness is the sting of the pain it caused, and nothing more. The broken pieces of our life, no matter how big or small, are only effective when they are used to create something new; again, no matter how big or small. For example, in the first chapter I mentioned how my wife responded concerning my dream that her hope that would be that whatever trying season might be ahead of us, that it would bring us two closer together and strengthen our marriage.

This brings us to the point of our brokenness being personal. But before I move forward with that, I want to preface the rest of the book here by simply preparing you for the fact that while I will illustrate a lot of personal experiences throughout this book as a way of driving home certain points, they may often come across rather vague. The reasoning behind this is not to undermine the experiences themselves or the impact of which they had, nor am I suggesting that you should take the same approach when sharing the stories of your brokenness and the way in which it impacted you. Rather, we want to be sure to place the main focus on how the brokenness impacted us and the ways in which we might question, experience, or even hope and desire that God will use the pieces.

Now, with that being said, there is a key element here that we must not overlook or become deceived by. The very first thing that we must acknowledge is the fact that while God may allow situations and circumstances to occur, He is a God of love, compassion, grace, mercy, order, and much more. Therefore, when pain and brokenness surface in our lives it is important to recognize that this is a result of a fallen world and our humanity. God never causes people to become broken, in His graciousness in giving us free will he may allow people to become broken, but He is never the cause of our brokenness. So, we have to be very careful, especially as Christians, how quickly we resort to blaming God when our emotional, mental, and spiritual lives are uprooted as a result of pain and brokenness. Lamenting and questioning God time and time again in these situations I believe is good because it shows our desperation and need for Him. But in doing that, we cannot blame Him for the fact that the world is broken and sometimes we personally feel that brokenness. This is why when I explained to my wife the interpretation of my dream, I was careful to say that I believe that God is going to walk with me through a trying season and not that He was going to take me through a hard season. Yes, words are important here, especially when we speak them into life. I had to make sure to remember that God wasn't going to be the reason for the pain that I was about to encounter through life's next storm, but that He was going to be with me through it all. Now, don't get me wrong, when the storm actually came, I had many weak moments when I blamed God even to the point of nearly walking away from Him, pridefully.

However, if God is not the cause of brokenness, how does it make any sense that He would give me a dream where I know that He was warning me of the fact that I was about to be broken. I believe that God was simply giving me insight into everything in my life that I had valued more than my relationship with Him. Trust me, this was a lot of things, and this is why the brokenness of the storm cut me so deep, I believe. I prayed the daring prayer of sincerely wanting God to lead me into the assignment that He has placed me on earth to fulfill, completely forgetting what Jesus teaches and told His disciples over and over again. *In the same way, those of you who do not give up everything you have, cannot be my disciples* (Luke 14:33, NIV). Earlier in the same chapter Jesus uses a hyperbole and metaphor stating, *if anyone comes to me and does not hate father and mother, wife and children, brothers and sisters – yes even their own life – such a person cannot be my disciple* (Luke 14:26, NIV). Although the word *hate* in that verse is not to be taken literally, the intensity of the standard that Jesus is setting for His followers is very clear. Furthermore, when I parallel Jesus's standard of giving up everything in Luke 14:33 with what we see in 1 Samuel 16:7 of the Lord looking at the things of the heart and not the outward things that people do, it is evident that the standard that Jesus sets of giving up everything to follow Him, starts with matters of the heart.

The matters of our hearts are so complex that we can't even understand them often times. The prophet Jeremiah even warns us, *the heart is deceitful above all things and beyond cure. Who can understand it* (Jeremiah 17:9, NIV)? David adds in the Psalms; *search me, God, and know my heart; test me and know my anxious thoughts. See if there is any offensive way in me and lead me in the way everlasting* (Psalm 139:23-24, NIV). I have learned in one of the most personal and hardest ways ever in my life up until now, that the personal brokenness that we encounter is a direct reflection of where our hearts desire once was or still is. I have also learned how in our religious circles we become so consumed with the need for our hearts to become cleansed and refined of the harsh or easily seen sins in our lives, then justify the idea that God is making us new since we are overcoming those specific sins, and thus our hearts desire must be in the right place since we are "sinning less." I have fallen into this trap so often as I have struggled through minor addictions and of course what the church views as the greatest sin of all, sexual sin. I absolutely do not want to speak lightly on sin, obviously it is detestable by God! Also, the church's disgust with people who get caught in sexual sin, not necessarily the sin itself, in my opinion; might be able to be partly justified when I read what Paul wrote to the church of Corinth. *Flee from sexual immorality. All other sins a person commits are outside the body, but whoever sins sexually, sins against their own body* (1 Corinthians 6:18, NIV). I took this quick bunny trail as a way of not only being transparent about the areas of sin in my life that I have had to work through, but to also reveal how I too became so consumed with this religious idea that spiritual brokenness is only a reflection of the harsh sins in our lives; or sometimes maybe the loss of a loved one to death. But after going through a season of life that I believe was solely dedicated to my personal brokenness, God revealed that for me the pain inherited due to matters of the heart, went well beyond this.

It wasn't until I was in the midst of the storm of my personal brokenness that I was able to recognize that the matters of my heart that had become deceived, way surpassed my actionable sinful struggles. Isn't it interesting that when we are in our small group church settings or even just talking with and confiding in fellow Christian friends, when talking about our weaknesses they are almost always directly correlated with the sins of action that we wrestle with? You know what I am referring to here; lying, jealousy, covetousness, lustful thoughts, you know, the basics. Well, when I walked through this season of brokenness, I realized that I was weak in a lot more areas then just actionable sin. And no, I am not referring to the weaknesses we might share with a future employer when asked in a job interview what a few of our strengths and weaknesses are. You know, shallow things like holding ourselves to too high of a standard or being too task or relationship oriented in our positions. Although these were absolutely weaknesses of mine, it went much deeper than that.

Remember, however, Paul's reminder to us, *for when I am weak, then I am strong* (2 Corinthians 12:10, NIV). Weaknesses are absolutely negative traits that should be worked on and improved daily, according to the world's standards. But according to Scripture, it is only in our raw authentic weaknesses that we can become strong because the only one we have to lean on in these moments is Christ. I just felt the need to reiterate that to remind us that as painful as it is to confront the depth of our weaknesses and brokenness, it has to be done if we want to obtain any true, life giving strength and Godly purpose.

The reckoning with our personal weaknesses, which are essentially the cause of our personal brokenness, lays the foundation of what it takes for us as Christians to get ourselves spiritually to the standard that Jesus expects of His followers, the giving up of everything! Again though, it is the giving up of everything in accordance with the matters and desires of our hearts, personally. Too often this teaching becomes reserved strictly for *the parable of the rich young ruler* (Matthew 19:16-22). So, it is determined that in giving up everything materialistically or at least having a heart that is willing to do so, then we have met this standard that Christ set before us. But the truth is, that matters of your heart or my heart that have not been given up for the sake of Christ might not have anything to do with the desire for materialistic things or monetary wealth. For many people, yes it does, but not for everyone. So, take a second and ask yourself here, what are the true desires of your heart? Seriously, at the lowest depths of your heart, and the core of your soul, what do you long for? Are they heavenly and Godly desires, or just good and moral desires? Yes, there is a difference! Are you striving to live in such a way that honors and pleases God, and God alone? The *God alone* part there is critical! According to the standard of perfection that Jesus commanded us to live by when he said, *be perfect, therefore, as your heavenly father is perfect* (Matthew 5:48, NIV), can you say with confidence that your name is *written in the book of life* (Revelation 20:15, NIV). These questions are not being asked with a judgmental tone, nor are they meant to bring you to a place of self-loathing or shame, but to truly consider, especially if you call yourself a follower of Christ or desire to be one.

I am a follower of Christ, and when I look back on that specific season of personal brokenness that God promised to walk through with me, I have to humbly admit that for me, the answer to all of the questions above that I just asked, were no. Sure, I desired to live a Godly life, but I interchanged the terms Godliness and morality so that I didn't come across too religious. Living in such a way that honored and pleased God has always been my hearts-desire, but I also always desired to honor and please a lot of other people and things as well, not just God alone. And no, I was not living up to the standard of perfection that Jesus set before us as his followers, and so maybe my name wasn't written in the book of life. I realized then, that I had never before been in a place spiritually throughout my lifetime, that I was truly willing to give up everything for Christ, especially not my family or my life like the above references from the Gospel of Luke point out. But in confronting this spiritual challenge of being whole heartedly willing to give up anything and everything for the sake of Christ, I discovered my core area of personal brokenness.

The area of personal brokenness that was at the core of my heart and soul was my childhood story. Now, I am not going to spend a lot of time here going into depth about it, you can read all about it in my memoir, *Longing for Identity in a Black and White World*. The long and short of it though was the fact that up until the age of nine years old, my childhood was very confusing in the sense that I was back and forth between two different homes; this meant two different families (biological family & nonbiological family), two different home structures (single parent home vs two-parent home), two different lifestyles (inner city living vs suburban living), two different racial demographics (African American biological family & Caucasian nonbiological family), and much more. This was not a foster care situation, or anything set up by the state or local government, just an arrangement between my biological mother and would be adoptive parents. But if it could be compared to split custody circumstances, it would have been 50/50 living arrangements as I spent an equal amount of time with my biological family as I did with my nonbiological. Again, this went on from the time that I was six weeks old until I was nine years and six months old. I eventually gained physical stability after my biological mother died and I moved in permanently with my other family. But anyway, like I said, my entire childhood story is written in my memoir. However, the personal brokenness that I had to reckon with as a result of my childhood experiences was my idolization of the "idea" of family and also human to human relationships.

There is no doubt in my mind that God gives us families and close friendships because he has created us for relationships and harmony with one another. Even at the beginning of creation God said, *it is not good for man to be alone. I will make a helper suitable for him* (Genesis 2:18, NIV). But one thing that I have discovered from my childhood, and in learning from others who come from "visibly" broken families, is how we promise ourselves that things are going to be different with our family. Furthermore, in our sincere attempt to show gratitude towards those who helped us along the way in our physical brokenness, whether it be a mentor who became more like a parent figure, a coach who we allowed to replace our father if we never had one, or our fostered or adoptive families that poured into our lives; we subconsciously begin place them on a pedestal, and if we're not careful they soon take the place of God in our life. No, as Christians, it's not like we're praying to them or worshipping them, but we could be living in such a way where we are honoring them more than we are honoring God. And when considering those who took on the role of parents we are absolutely justified in honoring them as the sixth commandment states, *honor your father and your mother, so that you may live long in the land the Lord your God is giving you* (Exodus 20:12,

NIV). However, the first commandment that God gives us is that *you should have no other gods before me* (Exodus 20:3, NIV).

I trust that I have always strived for and continue to strive to have a healthy relationship with my parents in a way that honors them but does not worship them or subconsciously allow them to replace God in my life. However, I could not say the same about my relationship or perspective on this whole "idea" of family, if you will. The fact that I experienced a lot of "visible" brokenness in my biological family as a child, as well as brokenness caused by the confusion that I sometimes felt from being different in my nonbiological family, family became my idol. I want to pause here and reiterate that we are talking about matters of the heart. Yes, I did have some gut wrenching physical experiences as a child that were unwarranted, but I can say with whole hearted sincerity that despite all of the hard times and confusion throughout my childhood, I never felt a lack of or unloved at all by anyone who was involved in my life, in both of my family's. So, when I say that family became my idol, I mean that's what I made it all about. I was going to make sure to be there for my children as a father since my biological father was never there for me. I was going to foster and adopt children since there was no way I'd be where I am if it wasn't for my parents doing that for me. I was going to teach my kids perseverance through the struggle since that's what my biological mother taught us, and my family was just going to be perfect in breaking generational curses and starting a new legacy.

Ironically, God has blessed me with the opportunity

to do each and every one of these things that I have always aspired to do in my family. However, in my season of personal brokenness, God revealed to me that He was at the center of everything and that I had neglected to acknowledge and express gratitude to Him for that. He is the one who placed the courage in me and my older brother's hearts to end the cycle of fatherless children, because without that type of courage that legacy of brokenness would have continued. I honor and I am incredibly thankful for the life that my parents gave me. But one of the hardest things that I ever had to say out loud in my prayer life was, God I know that it was all you and mom and dad were merely humbly obedient in being the vessel that you used. My wife and I have had seven children come in and out of our home through foster care and currently have two adopted daughters. God revealed to me the same exact message, that ultimately, they are all His children, not just our daughters that are not biologically ours, but also our three biological children as well. He is merely entrusting my wife and I with them for a period of time with the assignment of *training them up in the way they should go* (Proverbs 22:6, NIV). Then at some point, in His perfect timing, it will be our duty to release them. I say again with sadness but sincerity, our children are not ours, but the Lord's. Finally, God made it very clear to me through strong conviction and laying some of my sins bare before me, that He was going to be the only way that our family would persevere through challenging times and breaking generational curses to receive His blessings. It was going to have nothing to do with the way in which I lead my home because without Him, our home is doomed to collapse. It is quite incredible how something as cherished and loving as family and unity, can be at the root of our personal brokenness if esteemed and elevated in a way that is higher than God in our life. These are the areas in our life that we are referring to when we say that our personal weaknesses, which cause our personal brokenness, can go much deeper than sins of physical action.

Sins of physical action are obviously wrong and need to be repented of and processed through if it's a problem. Every day I have to be proactive in processing through my past sexual sins and addictive tendencies therein. Because if I am not, I open up a door giving the enemy a place to sit and mock me with temptation until eventually I fall short again. In the later chapters I will show you how going through the hard storms of personal brokenness makes you more vulnerable and although I did not stumble into areas that I have in the past, I opened gateways to it, but by the grace of God did not get caught back up in that vicious cycle of addiction. However, the point that I am trying to make here, is that my idolization of the "idea" of family and making the honorability of it a god to me, was just as great of a sin in my life as sexual immorality. The physical consequences are obviously a lot different, but both sins were keeping me from going deeper in my relationship with God. When I think about the first book that I wrote, *Longing for Identity in a Black and White World*, I realize how I talk a lot about both of these very topics, obviously because of the impact they've had on my life. The problem is, however, is that so much of the focus was on family and my personal struggles and not nearly enough on God's compassion for me through it all. I made it all about me. I am thankful for and trust that God was gracious enough to use the message of that book to inspire people as it was my testimony and biblically speaking, *you triumph by the blood of the Lamb and the word of your testimony* (Revelation 12:11, NIV). But thinking back, I do not think it was by accident that my season of personal brokenness was going on through the release of my first book *Longing for Identity*, the adoption of my daughters, and other circumstances directly related to family affairs and struggles that I was still personally working through. It was all happening at once, I believe because God was serious about wanting an authentic relationship with me that met the standard that Jesus gave to us in His Word.

You will seek me and find me when you seek me with all your heart (Jeremiah 29:13, NIV). My season of personal brokenness was the hardest season that I have ever been through up until this point in my life. But I remember back in 2008 when a friend of mine told me that they had a word for me from God and read the passage above from Jeremiah. The hardest season of my life gave me the courage, out of desperation, to seek God with all of my heart.

What about you? Do you believe that you are seeking God with all of your heart? Is there anything keeping you from going deeper in your relationship with Him? What lies at the core of your personal and spiritual brokenness? Maybe you're like me and have always idolized the "idea" of family because of the brokenness you witnessed in your own. Or maybe the opposite, you've idolized it because of the high expectations that were always present in yours.

Perhaps it's something so deep and personal that you don't believe anyone else could ever relate to it. I doubt this is the case, but even if it is, it does not matter because there is absolutely nothing that our Heavenly Father cannot relate to. *For he knows the secrets of the heart* (Psalm 44:21, NIV) and loves us all unconditionally. *Are not five sparrows sold for two pennies? Yet not one of them is forgotten by God. Indeed, the very hairs of your head are all numbered. Don't be afraid; you are worth more than many sparrows* (Luke 12:6-7, NIV). We are worth so much more to God than our human minds can even fathom, and the personal brokenness that God allows us to go through is the very thing we need to get us to a place of desperation and unconditional love for Him.

As it is written, what no eye has seen, what no ear has heard, and what no human mind has conceived – the things God has prepared for those who love him (1 Corinthians 2:9, NIV). I referenced Craig Groeschel's *Dangerous Prayers* a few times in these first few chapters. I also referenced Psalm 139:23, *search me God and know my heart.* Groeschel challenges his readers by proclaiming that this is the start of your dangerous prayer life, asking God to search the depths and core of your heart and soul. However, if you have never prayed dangerously on purpose, I would start by mediating on the Scriptures of God's promises about who you are, who He says you are, the love that he has for you, and the perfect and unique plans that he has in store for your life and eternity thereafter. This will help you to stay grounded, just like we discussed earlier in the chapter, it will allow your heart and mind to be in the right place spiritually, so that you can be broken effectively.

If you believe, you will receive whatever you ask for in prayer (Matthew 21:22, NIV). Therefore, because Jeremiah warns us that *the human heart is deceived* (17:9, NIV), be prepared for utter brokenness when you begin to pray dangerously the things that are on God's heart, especially when you begin by asking him to search your own. Without a doubt, spiritually, emotionally, and mentally you will become absolutely dismantled, torn, and seemingly defeated. Life as you knew it will come crashing down and you will feel like it has come to ruins; you will be shattered! Remember though, this is a result of flawed humanity and personal brokenness, it is not the will of God that any of his children should ever be hurt. But when you are hurting, when your life is broken, he will be there to walk alongside of you through the storm, so just hang on to him and keep pressing forward!

Weathering the Storm

When you go through the waters, I will be with you; and when you pass through the rivers, they will not sweep over you. When you walk through the fire, you will not be burned; the flames will not set you ablaze (Isaiah 43:2, NIV). What an amazing promise God spoke here through the prophet Isaiah! But I am not naïve, if you are reading this right now and you're in the middle of one of life's unpredictable storms that's leaving you personally broken, or maybe you feel like you're in the storm that's going to break you completely, I realize that a verse like Isaiah 43:2 seems pretty shallow and insensitive at the moment. Maybe I should have introduced the chapter with a Psalm of David; *why Lord do you stand far off? Why do you hide yourself in times of trouble* (Psalm 10:1, NIV)?

While you're trying to weather the storms of your life that are leaving you broken and shattered, it is completely appropriate to both stand on the promises of God while also questioning Him with desperation, from the inner most parts of your heart. But it is imperative that we do both or we risk staying in a sunken place spiritually. What do I mean by this?

The traditional Christian teaching that I became accustomed to growing up, and honestly the one in which I continued to live out and had begun raising my children with up until I went through the personal storm in my life that I thought was going to break me, was to *consider it pure joy whenever you face trials* (James 1:2, NIV). As a matter of fact, however, since we are to find joy in the trials, by default, they are no longer trials. Not to mention, God promised to *never leave us or forsake us* (Deuteronomy 31:6, NIV). Having a bad day, or a bad week, or a bad season of life was unacceptable and served only as a testament to my lack of faith in God; especially with all of the promises that God makes throughout the Scriptures regarding him being with us, specifically during hard times. I have found that a lot of the traditional Christian teaching that I have accepted honestly does a great job at acknowledging the supreme authority and power of God to get us through our seasons of brokenness, but completely denies the fragility of our own personal humanity in it all. In other words, we're not allowed to feel! We have to stand on the promises of God while numbing ourselves to how we truly feel about him allowing this dark season to surface in our life. The problem is, we might be able to deceive others, ourselves, and even our own hearts, but we can't deceive God. Therefore, he knows our feelings, the aches and pains that dwell deep within us when the trials of life overwhelm us, he knows when we are angry with him and others, and when we are slowly losing faith in him. However, even though God knows, it is still our humble responsibility to first, ask God to give us a heart with a clear conscious to protect us from deceit; and second, to give our entire heart over to God for healing and restoration, even the areas that are resentful and angry with him.

Being angry, sad, or discouraged at God about the brokenness that has occurred or is occurring in our lives is not a sin. I will say that again, it is not a sin to have ill feelings towards God as you lament and question him when the never-ending thunderstorms of your life seem to be no longer bearable. The most important thing to remember in these moments though, is the fact that you are still coming and talking to God about it. That is not a lead in to suggest that you need to know your place and therefore lament, question, and feel in a respectful and uplifting manner. If that is even possible when coming to God during life's darkest seasons. But recognizing and acknowledging the fact that when you are at your absolute lowest points in life, you default to turning to God. This should send you a very clear message. The message is that deep in your heart you stand on the truth that *God is our refuge and our strength, an ever-present help in trouble* (Psalm 46:1, NIV). Side note, I too find it interesting how so many outspoken non-Christians rave on about how they are just *going to have to trust God*, when their lives get turned upside down as well. Or, the kind of rhetoric that goes, *I know God got me.* Look, I promise that I am by no means attempting to make a mockery out of these individuals, I just believe that it is a further testament to the fact that God uses storms and shear brokenness as a way of reminding everyone, not just followers of Christ, that he is *an ever-present help in trouble* (Psalm 46:1, NIV). So, as you are weathering the storms, or the storm in your life that is about to push you over the edge, be raw and honest in your lamenting and questioning of God, but then listen as he responds with the truth of his promises. If you can't hear him, which is so often the case when we are in our fragile and broken human state of mind during these storms; open up his Word and read and speak the promises over your life. The Word of God, according to Scripture, *will not return to me empty* (Isaiah 55:11, NIV).

It was in fact my fragile and broken human state of mind when I realized that it is okay to be raw and honest with God as I asked him question after question with complete anger and sadness. I did so in desperation as I was trying to weather the stormy season of my personal brokenness. The circumstances that pushed me over the edge and lead me into my season of personal brokenness, was the black lives matter movement in 2020. Hear me out here, you have my word that I am not going to get too political at all. If you remember in the last chapter, I referenced my memoir *Longing for Identity in a Black and White World*, and I mentioned how one key element of my story is the fact that I was raised in two different racial demographics. I had my biological African American family growing up as well as my what would become my adoptive Caucasian family. Well, technically not adoptive because I never took on their last name, but nonetheless they are family. But to make a long story short, racial identity was something that I wrestled with a lot as a child because of this. Not racial identity in the sense of not wanting to be black and/or wishing I was white, but racial identity in the sense that as a young child I was torn between the loyalty of my two homes and families, and because one was black and one was white I made it about race in my emotional psyche. Also, in referencing chapter two again, I explained that the area of personal brokenness that I had to reckon with, that was impacting the depth of my relationship with God, was my idolization of the "idea" of family and also human to human relationships. As I sit here now, writing, in the aftermath of the storm, if you will; I can reflect back and see clearly how God used the intensity of the black lives matter movement of 2020 to bring these heart issues to the surface in my life. What most people in my home country of America and probably most countries around the world saw as a division in the States or a brewing race war, I internalized as a division in my family.

This idea of my family being divided was obviously not physical in nature. It's not like my black biological family and my white adoptive family were on bad terms or at odds with each other. But for some reason, the rhetoric used on both sides of the political spectrum was cutting me deep to my core, and I sincerely believe now that the type of impact that it had on me was God's way of helping me to search my own heart. When I heard rhetoric opposing the black lives matter movement, in the name of not supporting a corrupt organization of course; all I could seem to process was that black lives didn't matter. Or at the very least, the lives of black people who did not obey the law or law enforcement. Which at any time, in a moment of weakness, could be anyone in my biological family, too including my children as they got older. Furthermore, I was deeply discouraged by the silence of so many people in my white conservative community; on behalf of black lives. I trust and know that majority of the silence came from a place of not wanting to get political. But again, internally for me, it was not a political matter and I sincerely began to question how the black lives of myself and my children were viewed. Perhaps we didn't matter, or wouldn't matter, if our socioeconomic class was different. Conversely, I heard a lot of rhetoric demeaning white men, like my dad; and even over generalized statements claiming that white conservatives were inherently racist. Now, the truth is that at the core foundation of the social fabric of America was the false narrative that white men were the superior race and gender and that all black people were less and/ or second-class citizens. So, I absolutely believe that there are a lot of eternal consequences that we as a country are living with as a result of this. A key one being the fact that because foundationally in America, black people were considered less, that there have been many inherent biases developed towards people of color, in the United States. Historically, there is no denying this fact, but this is not the rhetoric that was impacting me on a personal level. Rather, it was the rhetoric that suggested that white conservatives where racist in a demeaning and hateful way. In other words, that they literally did not believe that black lives mattered. Mind you, we are talking about a white conservative culture and world that I predominately grew up in, so this too inflicted a level of hurt that I had never experienced before.

I will quickly add here, at the risk of being called out, that the rhetoric I used and stance I took, politically speaking; was the fact that black lives matter, because our lives do matter. As a Christian, proclaiming this fundamental truth on behalf of a black community that was hurting and mourning in 2020 seemed so basic and elementary. After all Scripture clearly states, *rejoice with those who rejoice;* **mourn with those who mourn** (Romans 12:15, NIV). However, because our country has become so consumed by political and media agendas, so many Christians had a hard time doing so in fear of being labeled a Marxist, or supporting the destruction of cities, or supporting an organization that desired to *disrupt the nuclear family structure.* As a follower of Christ, I would never get behind violence as a form of protest, I would never support an organization like BLM, and yes, the truth is that all lives matter. But in 2020, I will unashamedly and humbly confess that our black community was hurting and longed for support, which we would have strongly felt, simply if more of our fellow Christians had not been too ashamed to proclaim the fundamental truth, that black lives matter! Okay, I promised not to get too political, so I am done. I just felt that it was only right to be transparent regarding the stance that I took and how it would have been perceived politically. However, I can sincerely say that the stance that I took had nothing to do with politics, nor did the feelings I had regarding all of the rhetoric and opposing views, politically speaking. Internally, for me, the whole thing was making a mockery of my family, my childhood, and my life.

As I internalized what I felt as a mockery of the essence of my being and the life that I lived I became so angry. The lamenting and questioning of God out of utter discouragement commenced. I asked God why he would even give me such a life that was full of confusion, anxiety, adaptation, and a flawed identity. Especially if it was going to end the way that I felt it was coming crashing down. No, I do not mean physically, and I do not want to seem as though I was suicidal, I had just never felt so alone before in my life. I realized in my cries, pleas, and sometimes even swearing at God, that there was literally no one in my life that could even begin to understand the emotional, psychological, and spiritual dilemma that I was in. Not my parents, not my wife, none of my siblings, absolutely no one. At this point I started to become bitter towards God for giving me the type of two-family structure that he did, considering the fact that I literally had no family members that could empathize with what I was dealing with. I distinctly remember coming to a point in the summer of 2020 when I told God that the only reason, I am staying in my relationship with him, is because I knew that he had been gracious in forewarning me that this dark and lonely season was going to come. I was not happy about it, and I absolutely was not considering it pure joy, but I told God that I would try my best to hang on to him but that he was absolutely going to need to hold me because otherwise it was over. And I am so glad that he did, because you know what they say, things have to get worse before they get better.

Emotionally and psychologically the hardships just increased more and more. Anytime I tried to have conversations with people about what they viewed as political matters, but I viewed as family matters, resulted in intense conflict. I can probably count on one hand the amount of people in my white conservative circles who actually took the time to stop and sincerely listen with intent and respect, to my perspective as a black man with five black children, why the fact black lives matter was important to me. In hindsight, it seems like it should have been a no brainer. Furthermore, hearing people from my own racial demographic outright accuse my white family and friends of being racist, fueled even more anger inside of me. Looking back now I am able to recognize clearly what was happening. Although in my heart I felt alone and knew that God was the only one who understood me, in my actions I was defaulting to the very matters of my heart that God was working to restore me of, my idolization of the "idea" of family and human to human relationships.

Like I said, I felt very unheard and misunderstood by so many people. I do not believe that this was completely intentional, although there were many times when the white conservative voices around me, made it very clear that I had no right to play the victim as a black man. As a matter of fact, considering the white influence in my life, I should just be thankful and consider myself privileged. Seemingly suggesting that the only reason I met their level of success and expectation as a black man, is because of the influence of my white world. To be completely honest, I have never in my life felt so humiliated and insulted by such a worldview. I realized then, that subconsciously, to many people, my worldview and perspective as a black man was invalid unless it confirmed the worldview of the white majority in the conservative culture of which I was raised in. Suddenly, my black voice held little merit, because I professed the truth, that black lives matter. Remember, and I will keep reiterating this; to me, it had absolutely nothing to do with politics. This was the key aspect that everyone failed to recognize. Overall, however, I do believe that for the most part it was because people could not relate to me in anyway on how I was processing everything that was happening regarding the social justice movement. Now, there were a handful of people close to me and strangers, who eventually became our family's greatest support system throughout the year, who did listen to and comfort me and our family with a sympathetic ear during this season. But again, there was a lack of empathy because people just could not get it. I remember trying to have conversations with a few of my other black friends who were adopted into and raised in a white conservative world like myself, but they couldn't completely relate with the torn identity regarding family because they had never known their black families. Or, while they had been part of a white conservative culture for most of their lives, like a friend of mine explained it, "we still all had each other." Referring to the stability of his black family, despite being the minorities in their cultural setting. And of course, when trying to discuss these matters of my heart with my black friends who did not have the type of white influence or family ties that I had, the response most of the time was either suggesting that I express sincere gratitude to the people that helped me in that world, but that it was time to move on from that life since I was a grown adult now. Or, to find some way to hold them accountable for using conservative politics to justify why they are not proclaiming that black lives matter. Subtly suggesting that just maybe most people in my white conservative community did not believe that black lives mattered. Again, complete disregard and from my perspective, disrespect to a community that I love deeply.

Discouragement is probably an understatement to the way that I was feeling towards many people, even towards God. How could they not see where I was coming from? Everyone was well aware of my life's story, but still lacked the ability to provide an empathetic ear. There was little to no mental, emotional, spiritual, or moral support. With the psychological state I was in, I seriously have absolutely no idea how I persevered through that season of life. Furthermore, on top of this heaviness that I was personally experiencing, my wife was going through post-partum depression after having our daughter and was home alone taking care of our five kids. Additionally, as Norwegian living in the United States and our small community, she too felt misunderstood and unheard as a result of her cultural differences and her ways of doing things. But I know it felt different for her because she was all alone. She had no family or friends nearby her, so the feelings of being misunderstood and unheard, cut a lot deeper for her. In my heart and mind, when I correlated what I was dealing with in regards to the black lives matter social justice movement, and what my wife was encountering through her post-partum depression and unsure feelings of whether or not she belonged because of her cultural differences, I realized that although for different reasons, we were both experiencing the same challenges of feeling misunderstood and unheard.

My wife and I cried and prayed more than we had ever done before as a couple. I can't speak on behalf of her, but I am pretty sure that I talked to God more in the year 2020, than I had ever talked to him before in all the years combined leading up to that. I could not believe that this is what he had in mind when he spoke to me through that dream and we followed up by praying, God whatever you're going to walk with us through, we're willing and ready. Here we were trying to weather this storm as a couple with the assignment of taking care of five little kids, all at the same time. With the state that we were both in psychologically, I know for a fact that God had his hand of love and compassion over our children as well. I know that we were there with our children and loved them deeply; but sadly, I question if I expressed the love that I had for them in the way that I should have. Well, at least I feel that way because I know how consumed I was by all of the circumstances that were happening in our life, but maybe God's grace and mercy did not allow my children to feel that. Wow, my heart still beats with both gratitude and pain as I sit here and reflect on that extremely difficult season of our life that I truly felt was going to break me. I have gratitude to God for being faithful and taking us through the mental, emotional, and spiritual setbacks. I have complete brokenness that we had to go through this season of mental, emotional, psychological, and spiritual instability.

This most challenging season of my life was much needed, in correlation with my prayer of asking God to show me or lead me into His assignment for me, here. *Blessed are the poor in spirit, for theirs is the kingdom of heaven* (Matthew 5:3, NIV). Additionally, Jesus prayed, *your kingdom come, your will be done, on earth as it is in heaven* (Matthew 6:10, NIV). God wasn't specific with me in this season about what my particular assignment was, but he showed me that the assignment for every Christian was Kingdom living. It is our duty to live in such a way that displays God's will and God's Kingdom on this earth as it is in the heavenly realms. I will never forget a college professor of mine challenging us, saying, "if people can't determine or see a distinct and clear difference in your life, then you should probably question or reexamine if you're truly a Christian or not." As I continue to reflect on my shear brokenness as God walked beside me holding my hand through this seemingly never ending storm that my wife and I were trying to weather through, I can see now that in order to authentically pray Jesus's prayer of *your kingdom come on earth as it is in heaven* (Matthew 6:10, NIV), *we have to set our minds on things above, not earthly things* (Colossians 3:2, NIV). In doing so, we begin longing for, in desperation, a kingdom mindset, a way in which we can truly see past all that's happening in the world around us, and *seek first his kingdom* (Matthew 6:33, NIV). Therefore, in our desire to seek after and inherit the kingdom, we see above in Matthew 5:3, one of the only two ways to do so; becoming poor, broken, and shattered in our spirits. The only other way we see a reward being the kingdom of heaven in the beatitudes, is when we are *persecuted for righteous* (Matthew 5:10-11, NIV).

Brokenness and persecution are what we should expect, and I say nervously, what we should desire in this lifetime if we want to inherit the Kingdom of Heaven. Weathering through the storms of life is the only thing that is going to keep us grounded in God, *our refuge and strength* (Psalm 46:1, NIV). Also, let's not forget that the storms God will walk alongside of us through are personal and matters of our own hearts.

So, in the previous chapter we were challenged to search the matters of our own hearts to determine what was at the core of our own personal and spiritual brokenness. Where indeed we needed to be brought to a poor state spiritually as a way of going deeper with God. Like I keep saying, mine was idolizing the "idea" of family and human to human relationships; so, God did not cause, but allowed and walked with me through a long and dark season that I felt more alone than I had ever felt in my entire life. But his faithfulness brought me through it, and I can see all of the little ways in which he was faithful and helped me to be comforted and accompanied, in a season when all I felt was restless and lonely. In the next chapter we will examine ways to discern God's voice while weathering your storms.

But before we get there, I want you to take some time and reflect on the past or current storm(s) of your life. Although we have already challenged ourselves to look at the matters of our own hearts, the fact of the matter is that we are all flawed human beings and sometimes are unable to discern these matters appropriately. However, God is faithful and can and will reveal them to us, often in these storms that we are trying to persevere and weather through. So, if you have taken seriously the time to sincerely search the matters of your own heart but cannot seem to discern anything that you feel is significant, consider the storms, or the storm of your life.

What areas of your life are impacted the most when the harshest storms hit you? Is it never ending relationship conflicts? Is it resurfaced addictions? Do you go to a dangerous place mentally of not feeling like your enough for anyone, or God? What are the things that fuel your anger in these moments? What are the things that make you cry through these moments? Or, what are the things that cause you to become closed off, numb, and ignorant of your true feelings?

If we can be honest with ourselves about what these things and the areas of our life that seem to be influenced or impacted the most with these storms, we will very likely be closing in on what matters of our hearts that we need to let go of as a means of going deeper in our relationship with God. When you do finally hand it over to him, and I will say that if you are already in the midst of the storm anyway, you probably have very little to lose at that point by giving God full control. Or, maybe I am wrong about that. But handing it to God, will put you in the most vulnerable, scary place that you have ever been at in your entire life, but it's the best place to be because at this point the only one you can count on is God. Be encouraged by God's command to Joshua, *be strong and courageous. Do not be afraid; do not be discouraged, for the*

Lord your God will be with you wherever you go (Joshua 1:9, NIV).

I know, especially if you're in the midst of weathering your storm now, or like me, you still feel the shock of what that storm felt like, there is no way you can't be afraid, and you are absolutely discouraged. I couldn't relate to that part of Joshua 1:9 during my season of personal brokenness either, but I can promise you that the end of the verse stands true! God was, and God is, or God will be with you when you are weathering your storms. As a follower of Christ who still hurts deeply from the storm that broke me and maybe even might have killed me physically if I would have catered to my mental state instead of my spiritual one, I can promise you with surety, that the Lord God will be with you all the way through until the end.

This promise will be very hard to see when you are at the center of the storm and see absolutely no way out no matter which way you look. However, if instead of constantly looking for a way out, we keep looking for God even in his silence, and seeming distance, we will find him! *Be strong and courageous. Do not be terrified because of them, for the Lord your God goes with you; he will never leave you, nor forsake you* (Deuteronomy 31:6, NIV). Hang on to these promises as you are weathering the storms in your life that you deeply feel are going to break you.

I love these comforting song lyrics - I *can hear it in the crackle of a bonfire, and I can hear it in the middle of the ocean water, it's the voice of God, it can make a grown man cry* (Dante Bowe; Chandler Moore; Steffany Gretzinger, Voice of God).

In the weathering of your life's greatest storms, when God seems so far away, when you feel he is ignoring you with silence; just pause, feel, and listen, he is there, he is speaking, he will take you through!

Discerning God's Voice in the Storm

Whoever belongs to God hears the words of God. The reason you do not hear is that you do not belong to God (John 8:47, NIV). Oh man! This sure is a comforting verse to reminisce on when you're sitting shattered in the midst of your storms and trials. Not! Sorry, I guess I am on a roll now introducing chapters with complete insensitivity to the fact that the very theme of this book is personal spiritual brokenness. Sincerely, I did not open up with the above verse from John chapter eight for you to question whether you belong to God or not since you're having trouble hearing his voice in your storm. You do belong to God, we all do! Furthermore, I am willing to bet on the fact that even in your darkest moments when God is seemingly distant and silent no matter how much you're calling on His name, you actually are hearing His voice. The disconnect is that we have trouble listening because we are so distracted and consumed by the fire that we're in, and in that we begin to lack spiritual discernment.

In the midst of the fire and trials that we find ourselves in, if we lose track of our spiritual discernment, we are in great eminent danger. *Dear friends, do not believe every spirit, but test the spirits to see whether they are from God, because many false prophets have gone out into the world* (1 John 4:1, NIV). One of my favorite spiritual gifts, if I am allowed to have a favorite one, is the gift of prophecy. I remember in the past being in prayer and worship sessions and just knowing that the Spirit of God was present in the room. It was always the prayers that turned into songs and the songs that turned into prophetic words that made those experiences with God for me, so real. Maybe it was the realization for me that God still speaks prophetically through people just like he always has. Of course, it was always extra encouraging when there were prophetic words and truth spoken over me and into my life. I do not feel as though I necessarily made an idol out of this, but I can admit that over the years whenever I needed some spiritual encouragement I would reach out to friends of mine who I knew had the spiritual gift of prophecy, for prayer, hoping for a word from the Lord. Most times it was a powerful prayer and words of encouragement, never any word on my *calling*. Anyway, I remember early on during my season of personal brokenness, hearing God tell me very clearly that I was not to reach out to anyone for anything except prayer. It was not anyone else's job to hear the voice of God for me, he was going to teach me to discern his voice myself. But then he went silent, or so I thought.

Seriously, I did not hear God telling me anything. My wife and I prayed, and we prayed, and we prayed some more. I even took out some old church hymnal books and sang, because again, I find joy in singing old hymns! I found myself singing; *oft the way to the goal seems so weary and long, trials almost take away our song. Then we sigh and we cry, and we ask, Father why does this life my wishes all deny* (Barbara, Marvin, Marjorie Nichols; My Ways Are Not Your Ways). But I am telling you, I was singing this song from the depths of my heart. I was pleading with God to make it all make sense. But still, I felt ignored by God, but I did not relent in my prayer life and singing. They were literally the only two things that I had to hold onto. My wife told me how she would literally just spend all day praying when I was at work, during that season of our life. We know, praying faithfully like this should not only be reserved for the dark seasons of life, but if you've ever been through a dark season, I am sure that you can attest to the fact that your prayer life looks and sounds a lot different. In the mornings on the way to work I sensed my tone in prayer going from being angry at God for the way that I was feeling, to saying over and over again until it became, my hearts sincere desire, *God, I trust you.* I had never been at this place spiritually before ever; I was desperate, hurt, and lonely; but I remember just having this awkward sense of peace over me, that I know was the Holy Spirit. I even got bold, knowing that I was in the place spiritually that God was able to work, I prayed and told God that if it is going to take feeling the sting of this hurt for a lifetime in order to keep me this close to you, I am willing. Well, the sting has yet to go away,

I don't know why I did not learn from the first time to watch what I ask for in prayer.

Prayer, that was it! I was sure that I was not hearing the voice of God, but he had been revealing truth to me the whole time. *Cast your cares on the Lord and he will sustain you; he will never let the righteous be shaken* (Psalm 55:22, NIV). God had been revealing to both my wife and I the importance of praying from the depths of our heart and soul, with longing and desperation for him. *A broken spirit, a broken and contrite heart you God, will not despise* (Psalm 51:17, NIV). God was answering by showing us the true power of selfless prayers. See, as hard as that season was, we had finally gotten to the point that we knew God was in control. But we absolutely didn't stop praying, we just prayed for other matters. We prayed regularly for the strengthening of our marriage, we prayed for our children and sang *The Blessing* (Kari Jobe, Cody Carnes, Elevation Worship) many times over, and our faith got so big that we even prayed for random little miracles along the way that God followed through with. It was long, it was dark, and it was lonely, but the power of prayer strengthened us!

God sets the lonely in families, he leads out the prisoners with singing; but the rebellious live in sun-scorched land (Psalm 68:6, NIV). The promises of God are so refreshing, *he sets the lonely in families.* Now, I do want to be careful not to send the wrong message across here. Eileen and I did have extended family that we were involved in community with during this trying season of our life. Mostly, however, during this season, due to COVID-19 and everything else, they were more of catching up type of relationships, as we're a fairly large family. Also, as mentioned before, neither of our parents lived in very close proximity to us. Nonetheless, God knew that while we were thankful for our extended family community, and while he was teaching me to let go of my idolization of the "idea" of family and human to human relationships, that he still did create us to *live in harmony with one another* (Romans 12:16, NIV). *Furthermore, as iron sharpens iron, so one person sharpens another* (Proverbs 27:17, NIV).

This was the other clear way that we were able to discern God's voice and see him in this storm. Some friends of ours invited us to a Juneteenth celebration at their home. Most of the people there I knew from the past as acquaintances, and it was also kind of fun because nearly everyone there, but not all, were mixed racially in marriage, just like us. Seriously, this was cool considering the small community that we were living in, it was exciting being amongst an entire group that could relate to us in this way, and not just a few couples here and there. Well, the group had so much fun that evening that we decided to meet up again, and then again. As we got together on these evenings and had our discussions, it became pretty evident that all of these couples, especially those of us individuals who were black; found ourselves dealing with a lot of the same spiritual, psychological, and emotional challenges as it related to our conservative community's response to the black lives matter social justice movement. A lot of these conversations that were had were very intimate, personal, and revealing. Out of respect for the integrity of the discussions had as well as respect for our friends, I am not going to get into the details or specific topics that were brought up. However, the over-arching theme was clear, exactly what I alluded to that was merely the cause of what triggered much deeper issues inside of me personally, we all longed for more Christians in our white conservative circles to boldly proclaim the fact, that black lives matter. The keyword there being *more*, there were a lot that were boldly proclaiming this truth, we just hoped for more.

The excuses and justifications for remaining silent became overwhelmingly burdensome. Many of us agreed on how some of the Martin Luther King Jr. quotes that were always just historical, began to resonate with us on a personal level. We had become discouraged by our friends remaining silent on behalf of black lives during this time and some of us, in many ways, even felt betrayed. It was so liberating to have found a group of people who although had different reasons and experiences; empathized with the same understanding as me, the reason that we were hurting so bad is because the movement went a lot deeper than politics to us. And so, when more of our friends boldly opposed the movement in the name of politics; again, we could only help but to question where they drew the line, did all black lives matter? Or were we and our children given a pass since we were part of their white conservative community?

There goes that word community again. I am incredibly grateful to God for bringing my wife and I this community of people during this trying season of our life. As uplifting as it was for me to be able to process with others what I was dealing with in my own personal brokenness, through these meaningful relationships, I know that having this small group of people gave Eileen a sense of hope too. She no longer felt alone not being from America as there were quite a few others in our group who also weren't originally from America. I need to add in here quickly though, on behalf of Eileen, that while this was a group that was life giving for her and us, that she never underestimates the intimate friendship that she was able to establish with one of my aunt's even before we walked through this challenging season of life. My aunt is more of the quiet type and probably would not want me going on and on about her, but her and her entire family were such an amazing and intentional support system for our family during this time, especially for our children. My wife recalls the nights she stayed in the hospital with her when she had to go back in soon after giving birth to our youngest. We both recall the days that she would just drop everything and go and help Eileen at the house, and of course her willingness to babysit our kids if something suddenly popped up. Eileen and I are so grateful to God for bringing those people in our lives, for such a time. We have genuine faith that these friendships will remain, unconditionally.

One who has unreliable friends soon comes to ruin, but there is a friend who sticks closer than a brother (Proverbs 18:24, NIV). Other translations suggest, *that a man of too many friends comes to ruin* (Proverbs 18:24, NASB). I am so thankful for God's faithfulness and provision for our family during this rough season of life, for bringing us just the right number of friends and companions. Friendships that last to this day, and although the proximity of these friendships have changed, specifically regarding location, the people that God gave the courage to walk alongside of us during that season will forever hold a very special and intimate place in our family's heart. In our season of greatest need concerning emotional, mental, and spiritual support; the Lord brought people into our lives who's love, and kindness proved that their faithfulness would, and our relationships would indeed be closer than a brother's. Finally, as I mentioned an aunt of mine having an intimate friendship with Eileen, again, one that will last forever because it was grounded in love and compassion, it would only be appropriate for me to mention the two men who I felt stuck closer than a brother too me as well during that season.

The first one that I want to point out is a gentleman that I worked with named Bryson. He is a few years younger than me and he and I went to the same conservative church growing up. We only had a working relationship, but I remember being so encouraged by the fact that I could talk with Bryson, a white man who leaned more towards conservatism (politically speaking), about some of things that weighed heavy on my heart concerning the racial tension of 2020 and my perspective of the response or lack thereof, of the conservative community that we had been raised in. I remember the long talks in the truck on the way to jobs out of town, and the days that I just went off to him in anger and frustration at what I called the insensitivity of people within our conservative community to a mourning black community. He never said a whole lot, but I could tell in his silence that he was genuinely listening and in all of his responses, that he truly cared, deeply. Like I said, Bryson and I only had a working relationship, we did not hangout outside of work nor did I ever talk with him outside of work. But the working relationship that I formed with Bryson I realize now was God's way of softening my heart towards the white conservative community that I was a part of. I had been growing bitter, resentful, and even hateful towards an entire community of people strictly based off of my feelings without ever really having any meaningful conversations with others from my community. I had debates and disagreements, but very little meaningful discussions, until Bryson and I began conversing on these topics. Bryson may not have seen it then, or may not even know it to this day, but if you are reading this Bryson, I hope you are encouraged by the fact that God used your empathy, sympathy, and understanding in our conversations to keep my heart from becoming hardened and hateful towards community that I sincerely love and will always be incredibly grateful to God for. There was also my man Big John! John is a black gentleman and he and I go way back to middle school days and have a great friendship to this day. He and I have done some really bad things together, really good things together, and even cried and laughed together. John and I did not get together a lot throughout this season of life as he was on the road a lot with work and I obviously have a family to look after; but we talked on the phone quite a bit, and still do even today. I remember him saying, "Dixon, this is really messing you up." Okay, his language was a bit more explicit, but he was right. It is ironic though, in talking with John, I mainly expressed my utter discouragement with people in my black community who had been suggesting the inherent racism of my white conservative community. Again, to reiterate, it all impacted me significantly because the extreme rhetoric on both sides of the political spectrum was demeaning and offensive to people that I called both friends and family. But it was a relief being able to go off to him about a lot of the things that I was feeling, and if I am honest, in my humanity, it was often times me verbalizing it in the most non-Christian tone and choice of words ever. Most times, John would run with that energy and respond with what he thought I wanted to hear, but not necessarily what I needed to here. In the aftermath of it all, as we talk today, he says that he truly feels bad for that, but that he was sincerely concerned on behalf of my sanity during those days.

When I think about how John and I have been friends for just over fifteen years now, and still how much deeper and intimate our friendship got in 2020; and when I consider how the compassionate listening and kind words of my friend Brycen helped in keeping my heart from becoming filled with hatred and resentment towards a community and people that I love immensely and even acquired my love of singing hymns from; I can't help but to continue to reflect on Dante Bowe's song. It's *Catching up with an old friend, reminiscing on back when. Said it sounds like a choir, singing hymns, hallelujah, it's the voice of God, yeah, it can make a grown man cry* (Voice of God).

It was the passionate prayers, songs and singing, the community that became our family in our *season of loneliness* (Psalm 68:6, NIV), and the *friends that stuck closer than a brother* (Proverbs 18:24, NIV) that we were able to hear and soon discern the voice of God in the midst of our storm. And so, we are reminded, *whoever belongs to God hears the words of God. The reason you do not hear is that you do not belong to God* (John 8:47, NIV). Our family, most likely, like yourself, if you are still engaged in this book so far, belongs to God. It took us some time to discern while in the trials of the storm, mainly because we, or at least I, was listening for Him to continue to speak supernaturally or *in the tongues of men or of angels* (1 Corinthians 13:1, NIV). But as we listened daily to the lyrics of the *Voice of God*, and Elevation Church and Maverick City sing *Talking to Jesus* what I was missing became so clear. Especially as I began to personalize some the lyrics of *Talking to Jesus, My oldest is fifteen (my oldest is six), and I remember what that was like, trying to figure out the questions in life, I've been looking for a way to show him (her), how to make it alright.* Well, it took this hard season of personal brokenness that I now know that I am equipped to show all of my children how to get the answers to the questions in life that just don't seem to make any sense. *Just start talking to Jesus, just keep talking to Jesus, for the rest of your life* (Maverick City & Elevation Church, Talking to Jesus)!

God not only spoke to us and comforted us through this season of personal brokenness, but in bringing us to a place of desperation; we learned to pray from the depths of our hearts and in doing so have become equipped through experience, to teach our children to do the same. So even in our trials, God teaches us valuable and eternal lessons. I know that sounds just like a pastor giving a feel-good message, but in reality, cannot relate at all with your personal trials. Well, I am no pastor, and I can assure you that I am not pretending to be able to relate to what's at the root of your personal brokenness. But I hope that if you have been allowing the words on these pages to resonate within you, you can hear my heart in them. And so, while I do not know and very likely cannot empathize with the root of your brokenness, I can absolutely without a shadow of a doubt, relate to what surfaces as a result of it. The loneliness, the weeping, the sorrow, the resentment and bitterness towards people, the anger and questioning of God, the feelings of deafness and lack of discernment of God's voice, and the need to stay strong through it all, especially on behalf of a spouse or children. I do not know the roots of what makes you hurt, I do not know what surfaced in your life to put you over the edge, but I know first-hand the pain and affliction that you are dealing with as a result of it.

What about the pain and affliction? What is the result of that? Can you see or discern God at all when you ponder the pain that you are dealing with right now? I did not say, can you see God's goodness, or God's love, or God's graciousness; I said, can you see God at all, period? I saw God through my anger and resentment and like I mentioned earlier, thought about the fact that all of these great people of the Bible encountered shear brokenness on their path to fulfilling their God given assignment. But then I had feelings of discouragement and guilt for even comparing myself in such a way, and almost convinced myself that I was taking what was happening in my life too seriously, in other words, it was not okay to have feelings. Yes, I saw God in this too, because in criticizing myself in my mind, I was reminded of what God's word says about the importance of *taking every thought captive* (2 Corinthians 10:5, NIV).

Hang on to the promises in the Word of God when you're in a place, or in a season of personal brokenness. *All Scripture is God breathed and is useful for teaching* (2 Timothy 3:16, NIV). I remember hearing a pastor say one time, anything that you need to know about anything and everything, is found in the Bible. Seriously, we even tested him on this bold statement. "What does the bible say about using the bathroom?" *Designate a place outside the camp where you can go to relieve yourself. As part of your equipment have something to dig, and when you relieve yourself, dig a hole and cover up your excrement* (Deuteronomy 23:12-14, NIV). Context is important here, obviously; the point is, it's right there in the Bible. I could keep going on any topic, okay maybe that is still debatable, I do not want to get too side-tracked. But hopefully that verse gave you a good laugh and some comedy relief considering the intensity of the topic that we are discussing. But let's get back on track here. If you can find *almost* everything that you need to know about anything and everything in the Bible, then that means that the Word is the best place to go in your season of personal brokenness, especially when you are struggling to discern the voice of God.

That means when you can't hear or discern the voice of God, go read through the Psalms of David when he pleaded with God and even questioned God's faithfulness to him. *How long, Lord, will you forget me forever? How long will you hide your face from me* (Psalm 13:1, NIV). Find the Scriptures of encouragement when you truly feel as though you are in your darkest hours and just one more hardship will break you. Read God's promises of the Holy Spirit being your peace and comforter. In your long nights of sorrows and tears, remember, *blessed are those who mourn, for they will be comforted* (Matthew 5:4, NIV). When you're feeling misunderstood, or abandoned by the people closest to you, remember that even Jesus went through this when His time was coming to fulfill His assignment; *but this has all taken place that the writings of the prophets might be fulfilled. **Then all the disciples deserted him and left*** (Matthew 26:56, NIV). Nothing that you are going through is a surprise to God and there is nothing that you are dealing with that Jesus himself did not encounter. The only exception here is the action of sin, *but we do not have a high priest who is unable to empathize with our weaknesses, but we have one who was tempted in every way, just as we are – yet he did not sin* (Hebrews 4:15, NIV). Furthermore, while Jesus never sinned, *he himself bore our sins in his body on the cross, so that we might die to sins and live for righteousness, by his wounds we have been healed* (1 Peter 2:24, NIV). Therefore, he felt the heaviness and burdens that our sins cause us. So, again, there is absolutely nothing at the roots, or that surfaces as a result of your personal brokenness that God himself cannot empathize with.

God empathizes with our pain and he sympathizes through *grace, compassion, and love* (Psalm 145:8, NIV) in our brokenness. But I understand that these truths can be so hard to hang on too, especially in the middle of the storms in your life that are on the verge of destroying you spiritually, emotionally, or even physically. I know firsthand the emotional roller coaster of feeling as though

God is so far away. When we're talking to him, praying, and singing every day only for him to stay silent; only for us to lack discernment of his voice in the middle of the storm. But consider God's revelation to Elijah; *then the Lord said, "go out and stand on the mountain in the presence of the Lord, for the Lord is about to pass by." Then a great and powerful wind tore the mountains apart and* **shattered** *the rocks before the Lord, but the Lord was not in the wind. After the wind there was an earthquake, but the Lord was not in the earthquake. After the earthquake came a fire, but the Lord was not in the fire. And after the fire came a gentle whisper* (1 Kings 19:11-13, NIV).

Perhaps we can't discern what we think should be the voice of God in our storms because he is not the great wind that knocks us off of our personal mountain tops, or the earthquake that shakes us to our spiritual core, or the fire that we feel is going to burn us alive from the inside out. No, God is that soft, gentle, and kind whisper. That *still small voice* (1 Kings 19:12, NKJV) that comes when the storm **passes by**. And so, we must have the courage to be intentional about choosing to seek and discern the voice of God in the most practical ways, while in the middle of our life's storms. In doing this, remaining hopeful that at some point, in his perfect timing, we will again hear his *still small voice* (1 Kings 19:12, NKJV), and it will bring us great comfort and the words that he speaks over us in this moment will be *sweeter than honey, than honey from the honeycomb* (Psalm 19:10, NIV).

So, I ask again, where do you see God right now in the midst of your storm? What do you see being strengthened in your life as a result of the harsh pain you are feeling in this season of brokenness? For me, my marriage was becoming a lot stronger and more intimate every day. When I realized how my personal brokenness was rooted in my childhood story; the amount of love, compassion, and even protective instincts that began to fill my heart on behalf of my children, became inimitable. My protective instincts were probably even at an unhealthy level, and they still are. But I am praying about that. I finally learned what it truly meant to find joy in the little areas of life, since everything seemed so emotionally, psychologically and spiritually challenging at the time. I loved hearing our kids sing, *Fear Get Out of Here* (Crossroads Kids), after Sunday school; my wife and I smiled in our hearts when strangers would complement our children and make them feel special and not like an annoying burden. One time as we were walking into church, an older gentleman saw our five little kids, smiled at us and gave us fifty dollars on the spot. I remember how tight money was at that point and how timely that gift was for us. My wife and I would find laughter in the fact that our date nights consisted of making sure to leave late from my aunt and uncle's house (as we spent a lot of time there), that way the kids would crash by the time we pulled out of the driveway and we had about thirty to forty minutes of husband and wife time "alone" away from the house. We usually sat in the car in our driveway as well to continue our date, and also strategized about how we were going to get five little kids in the house without them waking up. God was there, he was with us through it all. He was kind in giving us strength, and faithful in giving us the ability to see, hear, and feel him even though, "we couldn't."

This truth is your reality too. Right here, and right now, in what feels like the darkest season of your life; God is with you! The strength that you are somehow mustering up to keep going is from him, the milliseconds of laughter are from him, the kindness of strangers is from Him. I know you can't see him, or hear him, or feel him; but I promise you that he is there, and he will see you through!

Find God's Blessings Through It All

Okay! You have officially reached the half-way point of this book! Seriously, I am very proud of you for getting through those first four chapters. If you are reading this and like anyone else, has dealt with hardships and trials in your life but nothing that you felt left you completely shattered, I am sure you don't see the big deal with having powered through those chapters. But if you're like me, and you've been there, or you're living in that season right now, I know for a fact that the heaviness of the words and themes within those chapters ignited a shock inside of you. A shock that may have triggered something inside of you taking right back to that season of life that nearly destroyed you, or just further weeping and heartache if you're in the midst of that season or the aftermath of it now. So again, I am genuinely proud of you for persevering this far through the book.

However, for a halftime break, let's switch gears before going full force back into the intensity of our shattered season(s). I want us to take some time here and consider how we can seek and discover the blessings of God through all of this. This is another one of those times that I sound like a religious guru being completely insensitive and ignorant to the hardships that you're actually experiencing. However, I am not referring to just this season of life that nearly had you committing spiritual, psychological, emotional, or even physical suicide. Remember, in the beginning chapters we looked at the matters of the heart.

We proposed that the personal brokenness that we go through, directly relates to the desires of our hearts that have become our idols and have taken the place of God. God revealed to me that mine was the "idea" of family and human to human relationships, I believe as a consequence of my non-traditional childhood. Hopefully, you have searched your heart too, and genuinely asked God to show you what are at the depths of it that is laying the core foundation of your personal brokenness; that will eventually lead up to or already has lead up to your season of becoming shattered. But in it all, there are so many blessings, small, big, and even unseen.

I shared how the racial tension in America as it related to the black lives matter movement of 2020 is what triggered the areas of my heart's personal brokenness. Before, I used to always just thank God for simply giving me a family. I was always grateful for my biological family and having known my birth mother before she passed away, and I was always grateful for the family that took me in and allowed me to be part of their own. As I mentioned before, because I have a black family and a white family, as a child, race was the way in which I always distinguished between the two. But despite all of the personal brokenness that was triggered as a result of that, in 2020, we were blessed with the adoption of our two daughters in October of that same year. I will be transparent here and admit that with all of the personal brokenness that I had going on in my life that I had chalked up to my childhood experience, there were moments that I questioned if we were doing the right thing as a family. Although the Bible does say, *religion that God our Father accepts as pure and faultless is this: to look after **orphans** and widows in their distress and to keep oneself from being polluted by the world* (James 1:27, NIV).

In adopting our two girls I was able to let go a little bit of the hurt that I was feeling from the heaviness of that year because I considered the heart that God had truly given our family for them. With this, I was able to parallel it with the heart that God had obviously given my parents for me. We had our daughters for two years through foster care before adopting them, but when I considered the fact that God had blessed us with the responsibility of raising them for a lifetime, I reminisced on the joys of my own childhood. I also thought about the sacrifices that my parents so willingly made on my behalf, and despite the personal emotional and psychological confusion as a child, the memories that filled my heart and mind were the happiness and joy that I felt in my home, growing up.

Additionally, we were also blessed with the opportunity to have built a good relationship with our two daughter's biological mother. We still have a relationship with her to this day and I am so thankful for that, that our girls will at least have that, knowing who their blood mother is. This is something that I am incredibly grateful for, that although I only had and lived with my biological mother for the first nine years of my life, I know who she was and can hold on to those fading memories. Not only that but knowing the friendship that her and my adoptive parents had and the stories that they have been able to tell me over the years of her life of courage and perseverance allowing me to obtain a view of her for who she really was.

Now, we do not have the type of relationship or friendship with our daughter's biological mother like my biological mom and adoptive parents had, but again, I see God's blessing in allowing everything to come full circle. Suddenly, I was able to see past the fog in the season of life that I felt completely shattered. God had a plan all along; *what was intended to harm me, God intended it for good to accomplish what is now being done* (Genesis 15:20, NIV). I was even able to obtain a whole new perspective on my personal relationships with each of my siblings, both adoptive and biological. In seeing both how well our biological children and adopted children established genuine sibling relationships, in addition to the confusion that went on for each one of them at the same time, I developed stronger love and empathy in my heart for my siblings in the family that I have become a part of. I always knew but never really let it resonate in my heart the sacrifices that they also made, in me becoming a part of their family, not just my parents. Furthermore, as confused as I was about my back and forth lifestyle as a child until finally being with them permanently, I was finally able to see clearly through what my oldest daughter was experiencing, the likeliness of my siblings confusion too as this had just as much of an impact on them. In having a new and clear perspective of this, God blessed me with a whole new level of love and appreciation for them.

As far as my sibling relationships in my biological family, on my mother's side that is, I too acquired a deeper love and appreciation for them. In the foster care system in Pennsylvania, or at least through the agency that we were going through, they do everything that they can to keep sibling groups together when they are placed in homes. I am so glad that our two daughters will always have each other to lean on in their later years when they will most definitely go through seasons of life when they will question their identity as a result of them being raised in our family, that is not biologically their own. My siblings and I were older than our daughters are now when we lost our mother and had to be raised in different family's, and the circumstances did not allow for us all to be raised in the same home, as a matter of fact we were all four separated. So, the extraordinary blessing in this, is the fact that God brought people into our lives way early on who had established great relationships with each other. As a result, although we were all raised in different homes, we not only stayed in contact with each other, but maintained and grew in our relationships with one another and still have them today.

Additionally, I mentioned above about knowing for a fact that my two adopted daughters will most definitely go through seasons of life when they will question their identity as a result of being raised in our family, that is not biologically their own. I know all about living an entire lifetime thus far wrestling with identity issues as a direct result of this in my personal life. For the first time, instead of just having feelings of the importance of processing it all, I can truly consider it a blessing now as this will be an area that I can sincerely empathize with my daughters in, from lived experience.

Furthermore, I am also able to realize how it was not only this type of parallel and reality of sibling relationships, or the personal connection that I feel with my daughters from similarly lived childhood experiences that we were blessed with through our foster care and adoption journey; but also the new relationships that we formed with other foster parents. If you are reading this and have been or are currently foster parents, I am sure that you can relate to the stresses and headaches that the system causes us so often. My wife and I were incredibly grateful for the foster care community that we were able to be a part of during this season of our lives as well, as their presence gave us strength in at least this area of that challenging time. The family's, the social workers, and of course the children were such an inspiration and blessing to us.

Additionally, for myself personally, God provided me with the opportunity to serve as a speaker for new, incoming foster parents through our foster care agency. The topic that I had the opportunity to discuss regularly was on *Transracial Parenting*. The main topic here was having discussions with incoming families on the complexities that foster children might go through when coming into a home that is of a different racial demographic. In the small community that we lived in, majority of the time this was children of color coming into the homes of white families. Looking back, I just find the timing of that opportunity presenting itself so incredible. The very thing that was at the core of my heart and personal brokenness, and in the midst of the season of life that I had to reckon and come to terms with it, God opened up a door for me to educate on it. Not as a person with a psychology degree, or as an expert on childhood trauma; but as a person who had lived it and was now in a place of brokenness from it. I suppose the artist Matthew West is right when he sings, *now I am just a beggar in the presence of a King, I wish I could bring so much more, but if it's true,* **you use broken things, than here I am Lord I am all yours** (Broken Things). What a blessing! I also had the opportunity to speak to a middle school and high school one morning during their chapel service. I just shared a little bit of my life's story by means of encouraging the young kids. Later, I was informed and saw that one of the kids referenced something I said during the chapel service in their yearbook as one of their "most memorable lessons from chapel." Again, in the place of shear brokenness that I was in, it was such an encouragement and blessing that in it all, people were not just listening to my words when many times I felt unheard and misunderstood, but they were actually being impacted by them. Proving yet again, that God can do the greatest and most impactful work within us, when we are broken.

It is only in our shear brokenness that we become whole heartedly humble. When we are at a place of sincere humility, we become little and fragile. When we are little and fragile, we not only see and hear God's voice in the little things like we discussed in the previous chapter, but we are also able to see God's blessings in the little things. So often we conclude that if we stay strong and hold on in our seasons of spiritual and personal brokenness, we can expect to reap a great harvest and an abundance in God's blessings. Well, our family has learned that if we just accept the fact that we are not strong and in reality are completely weak, helpless, and shattered in these seasons of spiritual and personal brokenness, we're able to find the seemingly little, but timely blessings of God, right in the middle of it.

Give us today, our daily bread (Matthew 6:11, NIV). We all know what type of circus the year 2020 was as it related to the COVID-19 lockdown. As a husband and father with five children, I was pretty stressed out when businesses started shutting down, as I did not know if I was going to be able to afford our family's bills. But God provided! I had two different uncles that I was working for during this time and the one closed up shop for a little while, while the other one had a government exemption. I was not a fulltime employee of his but just worked as a sub-laborer for him sometimes. I remember telling him that I completely understand if he needs to make his payroll workers a priority, especially as things were absolutely going to get slower. But in his empathy and kindness, he made us workers that had families to take care of the priority, while the other's waited out the lockdown on unemployment. I think I only missed one week of work during that time and our family was blessed with the fact that we never had to stress about taking care of our basic needs of food, shelter, and clothing. Seriously, as I am processing all of these little blessings right now that I did not realize God was in, I cannot help but to confess how much I took for granted and simply did not seek God in the little things before walking through this season. One more thing on this, just in case someone gets upset at me for working against the governments orders that year, we did have a government exemption that allowed us to keep working. I'll just leave it at that, like I keep saying, it's not about politics!

Sometimes it does take our seasons of complete brokenness to finally receive and experience the richness of the blessings of God. Where is God blessing you in this broken season that you might find yourself in right now? Or, if you're in the aftermath of it, reflect back and count the number of blessings that you might have missed along the way. In the words of Baby Bop off of the VHS tape, *Barney Live in New York City*, "I bet there are more than ten!" Sorry, like I said, I have fun memories of my childhood, and five kids under the age of seven, this kind of stuff resonates with me. Stop trying to stay strong in your spiritual brokenness and stop looking ahead to what blessings God must have in store for you on the other side. Admit it and come to terms with the fact that you are weak and fragile right now, that you might not make it through. Acknowledge how little and insignificant you might feel; only then do you open up your heart to receive and experience the richness of the seemingly little, but timely blessings of God.

When upon life's billows you are tempest tossed, when you are discouraged thinking all is lost, count your many blessings, name them one by one, and it will surprise you what the Lord has done (Johnson Oatman Jr., Count Your Blessings).

The Enemy is Lurking

Be alert and of sober mind. Your enemy the devil prowls around like a roaring lion looking for someone to devour (1 Peter 5:8, NIV). This is exactly why when you are in the shattered season(s) of your life, you are the most vulnerable and susceptible to the attacks of the devil. Because when you feel like your whole world is coming crashing down, it can be quite challenging trying to stay out of your head and remain alert and sober minded. I remember hearing a speaker one time reading a verse from Scripture but then adding one extra thought; *"you, dear children, are from God and have overcome them, because the one who is in you is greater than the one who is in the world* (1 John 4:4, NIV), **but greater is the one who is in the world than just you**." If there is one thing I realized about the attacks of Satan during this season of life, is that the enemy has way more strategies of attacking us then merely tempting us with sin. Don't get me wrong, this is absolutely a method that is used, especially if you are weak in the area of yielding to temptation. But in our minds, I don't think we can truly comprehend how evil and ruthless Satan is. I do believe that we give the enemy too much credit sometimes, almost as though he's as powerful as God just because he is in the spiritual realms. While he is not God, he is powerful and has absolutely no other mission but to *steal, kill, and destroy* (John 10:10, NIV).

The enemy's goal of stealing, killing, and destroying you is not figurative language here. This is Satan's literal goal and while the devil cannot read our minds, the things that we speak out in emotion and desperation during our shattered season(s) of life gives him exactly what he needs to start plotting against us. When I yelled at God in anger about how my two-family structure throughout my childhood and entire life, was going to be the very thing that was going to psychologically destroy me in 2020, Satan heard that and began plotting. My past sins of sexual immorality nearly wrecked my relationship between my wife and I even before we were married. It was only her heart of Godliness and forgiveness that allowed us to walk through repairing the damage that I had caused. In verbalizing my anger at God as it related to family, I began encountering strong temptations to fall back into the sins that indeed can and does destroy marriages and families. By the grace of God, although I did open up gateways through my viewing actions on social media from this temptation, I was able to stay clear of some of my past actions that have left scars on our relationship. I had to confess this to the Lord and my wife and while it did bring back a sense of fear because of the past hurt, I was humbly thankful for her continued grace. But like I mentioned above, temptation is just one of the enemy's strategies as he lurks around in your darkest season(s) of life.

Then I heard a loud voice in heaven say: now have come the salvation and the power and the kingdom of our God, and the authority of his Messiah. **For the accuser of our brothers and sisters, who accuses them before God day and night***, has been hurled down* (Revelation 12:10, NIV). Satan will bring every type of accusation your way when you are at a place of extreme vulnerability and insecurity. We also see his arrogance and pride in it, by doing it before God all day and night. I can see how this was happening to me when I had feelings of guilt during the process of adopting our two daughters. Furthermore, in the next chapter I will discuss how we actually made a physical change of relocating as a result of this season of transition in our lives; but even in this, felt the accusations of giving up too soon and running, just because things got challenging. Seeing how much more spiritually, emotionally, and psychologically stable our family has become as a result of the change that transpired from that transitional season of life, I am glad that we did not adhere to a decision based on those accusations.

Finally, be strong in the Lord and in his mighty power. Put on the full armor of God, so that you can take your stand against the devil's schemes. For our struggle is not against flesh and blood, but against the rulers, against the authorities, against the powers of this dark world and against the spiritual forces of evil in the heavenly realms (Ephesians 6:10-12, NIV).

This has got to be one of the most perplexed teachings of the Bible. No human mind can truly comprehend these verses of Scripture, especially when we are in our life's shattered season(s). When the circumstances around us are weighing so heavy to the point that we feel like we're going to lose it, we begin to rationalize and try to make sense of it all according to situations and what we are able to see with the naked eye. A lot of times this leads to blaming God and others, the very trap that I fell into. But *we do not lose heart. Though outwardly we are wasting away, yet inwardly we are being renewed day by day. For our light and momentary troubles are achieving for us an eternal glory that far outweighs them all.* **So, we fix our eyes not on what is seen, but on what is unseen, since what is seen is temporary, but what is unseen is eternal** (2 Corinthians 4:16-18, NIV). The enemy is going to be lurking at every single corner during your troubled season(s) of life and in knowing this, it is absolutely imperative that we recognize that every single aspect of what we are going through is indeed spiritual warfare! It is not people, it is not circumstances, it is not politics, it is not social justice movements; these are all mere disguises. The reality of what is actually happening is that there is a brutal battle going on between the *spiritual forces in the heavenly realms* (Ephesians 6:12, NIV), for YOUR very soul.

Consider this conversation from Scripture, had between God and Satan. *Then the Lord said to Satan, "have you considered my servant Job? There is no one on earth like him; he is blameless and upright, a man who fears God and shuns evil." "Does Job fear for nothing?" Satan replied. "Have you not put a hedge around him and his household and everything he has? You have blessed the work of his hands so that his flocks and herds are spread throughout the land. But now stretch out your hand and strike everything he has, and he will surly curse you to your face." The Lord said to Satan, "very well, then, everything he has is in your power, but on the man himself, do not lay a finger." Then Satan went out from the presence of the Lord* (Job 1:8-12, NIV).

The first thing to recognize here is that God is the one who challenged Satan on behalf of Job. What if in looking past our vulnerability, insecurity, and the things that we can see in our dark times, we had spiritual things in mind and considered that just maybe we are going through our trials because God straight up challenged Satan to a battle for our soul. We of course then see Satan using accusations against Job suggesting that it was only due to his physical circumstances that he stood strong in God. So, God released him to do what he wanted, and Satan began plotting.

Satan was on a mission for Job's life as he was constantly coming back to God and asking permission to act in ways that could ultimately destroy him. And while all of this was happening in the heavenly realms, Job and his friends were having a major gossiping session trying to make sense of the things that they were seeing. Paying no mind to the fact that just maybe there was a spiritual war going on. How often do we not do this when life becomes overwhelming and only keeps getting worse? Hear me, there is nothing wrong with seeking comfort in our healthy relationships during life's hard times. Furthermore, there is nothing wrong with having the hard conversations that need to be had, especially concerning the things that are weighing heavy on your heart. The prophet Isaiah even says, *"come let us settle the matter"*, *says the Lord* (Isaiah 1:18, NIV); additionally, *surely you need guidance to wage war, a victory is won through many advisers* (Proverbs 24:6, NIV). But if the war is spiritual and victory is won through many advisers, perhaps when we and our advisers (friends) come to settle the matter, the session(s) should only ever consist of putting on the full armor of God so that we can stand our ground steadily (Ephesians 6:13, NIV). In order to do so, we only speak truth in righteousness, we plan and act peacefully in accordance with the Gospel of Jesus Christ, we walk by faith and not by sight, and we stand firm on our salvation and adhere only to the Word of God. Then, we pray hard in the spirit (Ephesians 6:14-18, NIV) so that despite the many battles we've already lost, we win this war for our soul.

Remember, I am writing this in the aftermath of my shattered season. In the midst of it, however, I had a lot of gossiping sessions. Or even like Job's friends, nearly convincing myself to curse God, or at the very least walk away from him. But as I reflect on those times, in comparison with my sessions of spiritual warfare where all we could bring ourselves to doing was praying, singing, and meditating on God's Word; I hope and pray that when I encounter more of these season(s) of brokenness, that I adhere solely to spiritual warfare and not to the things that I can see.

There are many little battles going on and a major war happening for your heart and soul in the spiritual realms. I know that God uses physical circumstances to get our attention often times, but the only reason it is getting our attention is because at that point in our lives *we do not have in mind the concerns of God, but merely human concerns* (Matthew

16:23, NIV). And because of that, in our weakness and fragility we run scared and broken to God, which is exactly what needs to happen. At this point he can slowly begin to reveal to us his concerns, which are all spiritual and unseen.

Therefore, in recognizing that our entire life's journey is spiritual warfare, and simply that the enemy lurks more in our shattered season(s) of life when we are vulnerable and insecure, we can reflect on these lyrics.

This is my prayer in the battle, when triumph is still on its way. I am a conqueror and co-heir with Christ, so firm on his promise I will stand. I will bring praise, I will bring praise, no weapon formed against me shall remain. God is my victory and he is here (Hillsong, Desert Song).

"No weapon forged against you will prevail, and you will refute every tongue that accuses you. This is the heritage of the servants of the Lord, and this is their vindication from me," declares the Lord (Isaiah 54:17, NIV). Take a stand on this promise in your shattered season(s) of life. But do not be deceived in your interpretation of it; it says no weapon forged against you will prevail, or win. It does not say no weapon forged against you will not hurt you. Trust me, they will hurt you and bring you an amount of pain that you never thought possible. It also says that you will (future tense) refute every tongue that accuses you. In the meantime, stand accused and belittled just as Jesus was. Continue to serve the Lord through life's spiritual war and your dark season(s) and your inheritance will be great; vindicated, cleared of blame and suspicion by God! The enemy is lurking, but God and his army are fighting the unseen battle for you; stand on his promises, cling tight to his word, he is taking you through.

The Transition Within Transition

As Christians, we often hear sermons about how the transitional seasons of our lives are the ones in which God is preparing us for our next chapter. Additionally, these messages usually inform us of the fact that it is in transition that we will be tried and tested the most. Therefore, *let us hold unswervingly to the hope we profess, for he who promised is faithful* (Hebrews 10:23, NIV). When you find yourself in the shattered season(s) of your life, stay hopeful because all it means is that God is preparing and leading you into life's next chapter, and it's going to be a beautiful one. However, after coming through that transitional season, there is one thing that you have to be aware of, otherwise it will all be for nothing. There is going to come a time in your shattered season(s) when you are going to undergo the transition within transition. I am not even going to try and sugarcoat this in any way, you will know that you are in that phase because you will go from feeling shattered to feeling completely disintegrated.

Disintegration *is the breaking into small parts and pieces with the sole purpose of being destroyed. It is becoming much less strong and united and being gradually destroyed* (Oxford Dictionary). I know that we have been talking about the intensity of our shattered season(s) all throughout this book so far and have come to the conclusion time and time again that it is during these times that we are emotionally, psychologically, and spiritually broken. But I will put it to you this way, when you are finally on the other side of this transition, like I am now as I am writing this, you will look back on the transition within transition and realize that it was only God's love, grace, and mercy that got you through that last valley. In that moment; it was not your faith, it was not your obedience, it was not your prayers and singing on behalf of spiritual warfare, it was not your thankfulness, or anything else that has anything to do with you that saw you through that transition. The reason I know now, and you will eventually know that it had nothing to do with any of those things, is because in that transition within transition, you will not be doing any of those things! It was solely *God's grace being sufficient for you and his power being made strong in your weakness* (2 Corinthians 12:9, NIV) that allowed you to overcome that.

Weakness is probably even too strong of a word. I would say it was God's grace being enough for you in your mental, emotional, psychological, and spiritual *zombie* state. That's right, it will be in this transition that you will go from being broken and *poor in spirit* (Matthew 5:3,

NIV) to dead, *dry bones* (Ezekiel 37:4, NIV). In coming this far in your transitional season, it will no longer be that you can't hear or see God, because at this point you have taught yourself to do so in the simple things. Rather, in your crumbled disintegrated state preparing to be demolished, you will actively choose to ignore him as he is shouting for you while you are on your way to commit spiritual suicide.

While you are on the road to your spiritual death, the Father, Son and Holy Spirit will all start singing as a way of performing a miracle inside of you, *we call out to dry bones come alive, come alive. We call out to dead hearts come alive, come alive, up out of the ashes let a sea and army rise, we call out to dry bones come alive* (Lauren Daigle, Dry Bones). I know that I am dramatizing this in words on these pages, but when you actually live through it and reflect back, you too will realize that it was absolutely nothing ordinary that brought you through that final valley.

That final valley of your shattered season(s) is one of complete spiritual chaos and torment. Because remember, this is a raging spiritual war for your heart and soul. I think that it is the closest feeling that you can get to Hell, while here on earth as a Christian. Have you ever seen a movie where the main actor might be a detective or trying to figure something out? Finally, when they just about have it all figured out, the movie does like a runback or flashback, if that's what you want to call it; of the many events that happened leading up to that resolution. But it wasn't until that very moment that the actor was able to reflect back and see everything that they had missed along the way but was critical in getting them to their final destination. That is exactly what this final valley, the transition in transition, will be for you.

When you get there, in going through the hurt of running it all back with imagery in your heart and in your mind, as soon God's love and grace gets you through this last valley you'll be able to sing somberly, *I searched the world, but it couldn't fill me...then you came along and put me back together (through that awful season).* **The God of the mountain is the God of the valley** *(even that final valley of transition)! Oh, there's nothing better than you* (Elevation Church, Graves into Gardens)!

"For my thoughts are not your thoughts, neither are your ways my ways," declares the Lord. "As the heavens are higher than the earth, so are my ways higher than your ways and my thoughts than your thoughts" (Isaiah 55:8-9, NIV). It is only through continuously meditating on this truth spoken by the Prophet Isaiah that we can just slightly fathom how God came along and put us back together spiritually through breaking us mentality, emotionally, psychologically, and maybe even physically. The aftershock and sting of that pain still hurts, even now as I write, perhaps I allowed myself to relive it again, too soon. But take my word for it, if you can just hang on spiritually in this last valley, in this dark and brutal transition within transition, it will be worth all that was lost. Again, I know you are not really hanging on like you were before this moment; it's the final valley and you have nothing left to give. You have stopped praying, singing, and waging spiritual war and turned your focus back on the things that you can see. Therefore, when I say hang on spiritually, I mean don't allow the things that you see to get you to commit spiritual suicide.

What are some of the things that you are seeing right now? Shame or self-doubt, the disapproval of others, a battlefield in your mind, fractured relationships, mistrust for everything and everyone that you come into contact with, or perhaps the simple yet scary feelings that this is just the beginning and you have got a long road ahead of you. Let's pretend for a moment that this is the case. What if the road ahead of you is still long, and dark, and gloomy? But what if that is the *narrow road that you will eventually find life on* (Matthew 7:14, NIV)? Don't you want to strive your hardest to stay on it, no matter what circumstances might arise?

These lyrics really resonated with me throughout my entire season of transition even though I stopped singing in my transition within transition. *Is there anybody's sunshine, been turned to rain? Is there anybody's good time, turned out really bad? Is there anyone's happiness, turned out sad* (David Crowder & Mandisa, Let it Rain). Then, with feelings of hopelessness I sang from my heart; *let it rain, let it pour, Lord I need you more and more* (David Crowder & Mandisa, Let it Rain).

It is only in life's unrelenting rainstorms that we get desperate and speak seemingly insane things into our lives that we probably wouldn't otherwise; like, *"yet not my will, but yours be done"* (Luke 22:42, NIV). But like I said, in the transition within transition our spiritual compass is a way out of whack, and we begin to focus on the things that we see. Knowing this now, when I look back, I wish that I would have focused on the good things that I saw. That would be my encouragement to you, when you encounter the transition within transition and you are only focusing on the things seen and not unseen, that's when you can apply the humanist perspective and find all the positive aspects. On the contrary, if you have yet to go through this, start praying hard now for a spiritual lens during that transition within transition because *whatever you ask for in prayer, believe that you have received it, and it will be yours* (Mark 11:24, NIV). I wish I would have had this spiritual lens during our transition within transition, but I didn't. However, I trust and know that God was still faithful.

With the heaviness of our shattered season, we made the decision to move to Norway, my wife's home country. From the perspective of where she and I were at in our individual psychological states, we knew that it would be best for her to be close to her family, and I felt that I needed a mental break and distance from everything that was happening. Yes, even while we are here today, my wife and I admit that this decision was very likely made out of impulse and emotion due to how unhealthy we both were mentally, emotionally, psychologically, and spiritually. For example, she wonders how different everything would have looked if she had not had post-partum depression. I reflect back on the shear loneliness that I felt and how we made this decision before we really got to know and build intimate relationships with the new friends that we made in our Juneteenth group. Therefore, I too wonder how different that would have looked had we waited it out. But like I said, God is faithful. When I consider the miracle of all the logistics working out in us getting to Norway, how much healthier mentally, psychologically, emotionally, and spiritually that her and I are now personally and as a married couple; in addition to how well our children have adapted and are thriving in a new country and culture, I know that this is exactly where we need to be for this season of life. With that being said, her and I admit that we will forever be tormented by the thought inside of our heads questioning if we did the right thing by relocating strictly because life got extremely challenging.

Following through to come here was probably one of the hardest things for me personally to have the courage to do, whole heartedly. Like I said, neither one of our parents lived close by us, but my parents had been working on and have now moved back to Pennsylvania, right when we moved to Norway. This has been one of the hardest things for me personally to carry, as I felt like I took their grandchildren away from them. Every day I hope and pray to God that they do not hold resentment in their hearts towards our family for that. At times I feel even more guilty because in knowing that they are not my biological parents, I feel an extra dose of betrayal on my end for leaving them. I remember even before we left writing them and thanking them for everything that they have done for me, seemingly like a goodbye letter. This was one of the most unsettling feelings that I have ever had, for the first time ever in my entire life I made that disconnect. Not a disconnect as though we were no longer family, obviously we still are; but I suppose a disconnect in what God was trying to teach me, that I had to let go of everything that was closer to me in my heart than him if I truly wanted to walk in the assignment that he has given me.

However, when these mixed emotions and feelings come over me, I can reflect on the transition within transition season on something good that was seen. Despite all of those ill feelings of being unheard and misunderstood; in this aftermath season I hold on to the love, care, and sadness that my parents displayed to our family during that last and cruelest valley. I am thankful that today I can rest in the fact that in that time I did not have to question my parents love and relationship with us. I am thankful for all of the physical help that they gave us and their willingness to spend quality time with us before we left despite the sadness and possible betrayal that they may have felt. It may seem strange, and maybe not right, but I hold the images of the tears they cried when we left, deep down in my heart. Sincerely, considering the psychological state that I was in; I thank God for comforting hugs and tears of mom and dad. They cared deeply that we were going and were going to hurt in their hearts missing us, just like I would them. It has only been four months since we landed here over the pond and I miss my mom and dad more than I ever have before, specifically as I think about the years I spent traveling as a missionary and in the military. I believe that God is testing me and them in this too, as we do not know when we'll see each other again due to the COVID-19 restrictions.

Other positive things that I am now able to look back on and see, are the tiny, yet big miracles of God. We had a container scheduled to come to our house to load up all of our furniture to ship over here to Norway for us. We had absolutely no help, whatsoever! But the day that it was scheduled to come a major snowstorm hit us and they had to cancel. On the day that it was rescheduled, the tribe that God brought into our lives that season all came through for us. Friends from our Juneteenth crew, a cousin of mine, fellow foster parents, and even some of our kind neighbors who had been working from home and spared two hours. Call it a coincidence or simple delay because of the weather, but our family knows that it indeed was a miracle from God!

Then we had a lot of work to do on the house to get it ready to sell. We had planned on updating it a bit for market value by putting in new floors and painting. I felt some type of way about asking anyone for help since it was just to help with getting it updated to sell, but I knew there was no way Eileen and I were going to be able to get it done alone with five little kids running around. I humbly reached out to our Juneteenth tribe again, only offering payment of breakfast and lunch if they came a Saturday and helped us. Of course, they helped us with no questions asked. I am even tearing up a little right now when I think about their unrelenting support for our family that year, having only known us for a short while. I hope, trust, pray, and know that God will bless each one of them greatly for the major way in which they blessed our family that year. Of course, on this workday, my aunt (my wife's close friend) took care of the kids and sent us a bunch of food. Again, with her servant heart, I know she's got herself a great reward waiting for her in heaven.

Finally, in our transition within transition when I was full force looking at the negative things that I saw and just wanted to go, I can look back now and see the little moments of family time that we were finally able to have again when mom and dad moved back. We spent a lot of time at their house those last few weeks before we left and seeing them cherish being nearby their grandchildren makes my heart very happy, even today. My dad, my two brothers, and I went out for dinner the night before we left! We had not done that for a long time, and it meant a lot to me. I look forward to doing that with them again, maybe even here in Norway.

In the midst of all of this, came the time for the physical transition, when we left. We had to go on different flights due to the fact that we were even bringing pets over here. Yeah, talk to my lovely wife about that! But I remember when I was taking her and three of our kids to the airport, I just broke down. I watched my daughter have a meltdown with tears in her eyes as I put her in the car seat, and my mom hurting with tears in her eyes as well. I could not control myself, I immediately got flashbacks to when I used to have meltdowns just like my daughter was, when I would be going back and forth between my two homes as a child. I think that was the moment I "snapped out" of my transition within transition because I remember saying to God from the depths of my heart, "I sure hope you have a plan and will one day make this all make sense, because this is awful!" I had these same flashbacks two more times, once when I gave my dad a hug goodbye at the airport, and another time when my girls and I were saying goodbye to their biological mother on video chat at the airport before we left. I uttered the same words, "God, I sure hope you have a plan and will one day make this all make sense, because this is awful!"

"For I know the plans I have for you" declares the Lord, *"plans to prosper you and not to harm you, plans to give you a hope and a future"* (Jeremiah 29:11, NIV).

The Aftermath

Well, like I said, as I am sitting here writing this, it has been four months since we have been here at our new home in Bergen, Norway. I wish that this was the part of the story that I could talk all about how reconciliation has finally happened and that I finally feel like I am walking in my God given assignment, but that is not the case. However, in learning to walk by faith and not by sight during our shattered season of life, I am hopeful that each of those will come to pass. I can say though, that one of the first things I did in the current aftermath of that season, is deliberately disobey God in my heart. Remember how I mentioned that God made it very clear to me not to reach out to people for anything besides prayer. Well, I reached out to an old friend that I used to go to church with way back when my biological mother was still alive. I just asked her for prayer, but in my heart, I was hoping she would give me a word from the Lord as I knew she had the gifts of prophecy and discernment.

Again, even in our mistakes, in this case my disobedience, God is faithful. With the hope that she would reveal something extraordinary to me from God, in praying for me all she said was, "it's been a rough season due to a lot of people, but God will take you through and know that he has a plan."

I do know that God has a plan, I just wish he would reveal it to me so I can stop stressing about it. One evening though my wife and I were discussing that we always hear sermons and stories about God using peoples hurt and brokenness to create something new. The story is usually told with an analogy taken from Jeremiah chapter eighteen. *So, I went down to the potter's house and I saw him working at the wheel. But the pot he was shaping from the clay was marred in his hands; so, the potter formed it into another pot, shaping it as seemed best to him. Then the word of the Lord came to me. He said, "can I not do with you Israel as this potter does?" Declares the Lord. "Like clay in the hand of the potter, so you are in my hand, Israel"* (Jeremiah 18:3-6, NIV). However, my wife and I determined that the season of life that we were left feeling completely broken, for sure did not feel like we were clay being formed and reformed. As a matter of fact, we felt more like a family of fragile vases that were slammed relentlessly onto a concrete pad, left shattered with no remorse. What can God make out of that, what could he possibly make from millions of little pieces of shattered glass vases?

Then I did some research and it all made sense to me. *You are the light of the world. A town built on a hill cannot be hidden. Neither do people light a lamp and put it under a bowl. Instead they put it on its stand, and it gives light to everyone in the house. In the same way, let your light shine before others, that they may see your good deeds and glorify your Father in heaven* (Matthew 5:14-16, NIV). So according to this passage, I am to be a stand for God's light to be able to shine through for everyone else. But again, how was God going to create a light stand out of a family of shattered glass vases. Then I came across something interesting, broken glass votives. A votive candle is a small, slow-burning candle and because of their functionality they have to set in specific types of candle holders, which are glass. The process of making these broken glass votive candle holders is very precise and unique.

The preciseness of this process is the fact that the glass obviously has to be broken but have come from something that was at least sturdy, like a vase. Next, in handling each piece of broken glass with care, they all need to be placed in a confined space or box with a cloth draped over them to keep them in place. Then, the person creating the broken glass votive must take a hammer and begin beating on the pile of already broken glass, crushing them into tiny seemingly insignificant pieces. Next, you pile all of the tiny glass pieces into another tall glass container. Finally, you take a another already created glass votive holder that is significantly smaller so that it can be placed comfortably within the shattered pieces of glass in the tall glass container. After that you place the votive candle into the small votive holder within the broken pieces and seal the tall glass container with a lid. You turn the lights off in the room of which this is created, and the light that shines through this creation is extraordinary, especially when you consider the process of which it took to get there.

Maybe this was a symbol of the process that our family had to go through in that challenging season of life. Perhaps God had to spiritually crush my wife and I to the point that we had no other option but to be placed back in his presence. But that the reality is, it is only in being confined in his presence, and seeing the light of Christ shining through in our little children that we too have been able to receive that light for ourselves again and begin shining little by little. I suppose that is why *he said: "truly I tell you, unless you change and become like little children, you will never enter the kingdom of heaven"* (Matthew 18:3, NIV). Again, I could be over dramatizing the concept, but reflecting back on how we somehow came through that dark time, it really does make sense to me.

It has been interesting though, during our prayer and intercession sessions back home before we left, Eileen and I prayed a lot that God would open and close doors as far as what we were supposed to do once we got here to Norway. Specifically, regarding job placement and everything. At the same time, one word that Eileen kept hearing God say was *rest*. We just automatically assumed that meant resting from the emotional and psychological depressing states that we were in. But here I am four months in, and I am still waiting for a work visa and a stay-at-home dad, while Eileen is out working and the "bread-winner" for the family. In the beginning we chalked this up to God giving us insight on what it takes to fulfill the role of the other person, regarding how we were doing things back home with me working and her being a full-time stay-at-home mom. However, I actually think that this was God's way of giving us the exact rest that we needed, individually.

Eileen is resting by no longer being cooped up in the house all day with five kids running around and of course can breathe in comfortability again being back in her home country and culture and with her family after being away for nearly eight years. For myself, I wasn't sure how long it would take me to get a work visa once I got here so the year before we left while dealing with everything that we were spiritually, emotionally, and psychologically; I was also working as many hours as possible so that we had financial stability when coming here. So while I felt lazy in the beginning, I know that this has been good for me, and I have it easier than Eileen did as our oldest is in school now and three of the other four are in daycare, so I only have one kid at home with me all day.

Being home all day every day for the past four months has forced me to process everything that happened in 2020. I still have moments that I cry thinking about the intensity of it all and the shear loneliness that we felt, I guess it kind of puts me in a place of shock because I seriously cannot comprehend and believe that it all went down the way that it did. But in thinking about it all, I decided to approach it the same way we used to do after training exercises when I served in the army. We called it after action reviews (AAR), which included reflecting back on the training exercise and naming three to five things that were done right and three to five things that could be improved on. So, for example, during what felt like our shattered season, I trust that I did well hanging onto the courage that God gave me to ensure that I was putting my wife and children first in everything concerning the day to day tasks. As well as being sure to defend their honor no matter what. On the contrary, while this was indeed my actions, I know an area that I did not do well in was allowing my ideas of what the thoughts and opinions of others might be about me, not to influence me both emotionally and mentally.

Since being in this season of rest, I have read and listened to a lot of audio books. One book that helped me a lot when realizing my area of weakness in feeling the heaviness of the opinions and thoughts of others was, *Courage to be Disliked* (Ichiro Kishimi & Furnitake Koga). The authors argue that the root of all of our insecurities and personal limitations; are relationships, period. They break down the psychology of the fact that if we lived in a world all on our own where no one could ever weigh in their thoughts or opinions about us, our potential would be unlimited. Now, this book is a Japanese phenomenon using the psychological theories of Alfred Adler, not at all rooted in Scripture. However, when I considered my discouragement of feeling un-liked in my shattered season, compared to what Jesus teaches, *you will be hated by everyone because of me, but the one who stands firm to the end will be saved* (Matthew 10:22, NIV); I discovered that even just the feeling of not being liked is something that we all need to have genuine courage in, if we truly want to walk in our God given assignments.

Another area that God showed me throughout these last few months, is how I allowed my discouragement of feeling un-liked to impact my heart's attitude towards people. I read Philip Yancey's, *The Scandal of Forgiveness*, a month or two ago. He argues exactly what his title says, that the act of forgiveness is scandalous. Scandalous is defined as *shocking and unacceptable or even disgraceful* (Oxford Dictionary). Therefore, Yancey is driving home the point that in our humanity we do not even have the capacity to forgive because it goes against our very nature. It is scandalous. When I realized the depth of this concept and its truth, it dawned on me how freely we as Christians and non-Christians alike, often times just throw around the phrase "I forgive you" without any true comprehension or understanding of the magnitude of its meaning. I would go as far to say that sincere forgiveness from the heart is impossible to do unless the Holy Spirit is living within us. But we are taught, *and when you stand praying, if you hold anything against anyone, forgive them, so that your Father in heaven may forgive your sins* (Mark 11:25, NIV).

For the entire year of my personal brokenness when I felt shattered, I prayed day in and day out, but never once adhered to what we see here in the Gospel of Mark. I held a lot of things against a lot of people and it is because forgiveness is scandalous and not in my finite ability to do so. So, throughout this season of rest I have prayed that God would *create in me a pure heart and renew a steadfast spirit within me* (Psalm 51:10, NIV). I am thankful that God's grace kept me from becoming full of hatred and resentment in my heart, but I know that my discouragement and disappointment from that challenging season of life has kept me from forgiving. Daily I pray and ask God to show me his heart of forgiveness so that I can sincerely walk in that in all of my relationships. I have learned that we are not like God in the sense that we can't forget the ways in which others have hurt us, but we can obtain his heart of love for people and *love keeps no record of wrongs*

(1 Corinthians 13:5, NIV). Therefore, although we cannot forget the pain we felt, in having God's love in our hearts, we are able to actively choose to not hold that unforgotten hurt against others, in any way. I have also had to let go of my false humility and pride in the sense that although I know that I have hurt others and need to seek God and those of whom I hurt for forgiveness, I am still allowed to hurt and acknowledge the ways in which others have wronged me.

It is only with this type of transparency that can we grow in our relationships with one another. In Yancey's, *Scandal of Forgiveness*, he looks at forgiveness on a grand scale and determines that the scandal of it and thus humanity's default to unforgiveness, is the root cause of wars and political unrest. I perceived it from our interpersonal relationships and have concluded that if sincere and authentic forgiveness was happening regularly in our personal relationships, there would never be any conflict or relationship tension. But again, our human minds cannot even comprehend this idea of forgiveness; vengeance and getting even is who we are in the flesh. This is why Paul says, *you however, are not in the realm of the flesh but are in the realm of the Spirit, if indeed the Spirit of God lives in you* (Romans 8:9, NIV). So, again, if as Christians we live according to the realm of the Spirit of God, like we claim we do and are supposed to, we should never see brokenness in our relationships.

As Christians, brokenness in our relationships should not be the result of the shattered season(s) of life that we encounter and go through. Unfortunately, however, this is a catch-22 because often times it is the actions of others that cause our shattered season(s) and could be our own actions that cause others their shattered season(s). In the humanity of others, we can become hurt while also in our own humanity we can hurt others. Consequently, in our humanity as a whole, authentic forgiveness is a scandal; and so, the vicious cycle of pain, brokenness, and shattered season(s) continue. This leaves only one final ultimatum, Jesus Christ and his death on the cross and resurrection.

It has been a rough season due to a lot of people, just like my friend told me. How about for you? Are you in the aftermath of a recently shattered season of life and you're just trying to make sense of everything? I am telling you, that you absolutely will not be able to. I am sure for you too, it has been a rough season, due to a lot of people. But if there is one thing that I have learned, the absolute only way that we will ever be able to truly keep moving forward into our God given assignment, is if we choose authentic forgiveness of others. This is not contingent upon whether or not you've received an apology from others, nor is it contingent upon whether or not others know or even acknowledge that you have been hurt by them. Remember, when we have been hurt by other people and address its reality, the people who are responsible for hurting us do not get to decide whether or not we should be hurt by their actions. The same is true when we are confronted about the ways in which we unintentionally or intentionally hurt others, we have no say in the ways in which they have been hurt or feel as a result of it. But we are fully responsible for the ways in which we made them feel and have to do our part in striving to reconcile it and make the ways in which we have wronged another, right. However, again, our role in forgiving others is not contingent upon whether or not others forgive us, nor our questioning if others have forgiven us for our wrongdoings towards them. Finally, and this is probably one of the hardest things that we have to come to terms with; choosing authentic forgiveness is not contingent upon whether or not reconciliation ever takes place, especially when considering the forgiveness that needs to occur in our close and personal relationships. We hope, pray, and trust God that he can and will restore those broken relationships as he promises, *I am making everything new, for these words are trustworthy and true* (Revelation 21:5, NIV). However, should we have to face the reality that in our humanity sometimes our brokenness is never restored, specifically concerning our human to human relationships, we still must choose authentic forgiveness within our hearts. As Christians we have to choose authentic forgiveness, which only comes from dwelling on the Spirit and looking to Jesus Christ and the cross. *For if you forgive other people when they sin against you, your heavenly father will also forgive you* (Matthew 6:14, NIV). I do not think Jesus puts it in that order to scare us into forgiving others so that we are forgiven by God. I think it is put in that order because of his understanding of our humanity and love for us. It is impossible, I think, for us to search our own hearts for conviction of our wrongdoings or other matters of the heart that are keeping us from going deeper in our relationship with God, when the top layer of our hearts is that of the hurt and pain inflicted on us by others.

Only in peeling these top layers off through scandalous

forgiveness, do we provide a gateway for God to come in and do a work in us. In this aftermath season of rest, I have learned that so often the root cause of our shattered season(s) are people. It could be the emotional wounds inflicted on us by those of whom we are in close and personal relationships with, the hurt caused by those of whom we merely know as acquaintances, or even people that we do not know at all but have been emotionally or mentally crippled by their actions. But if people are often the root cause of so much of our personal brokenness, and many of our trying seasons; then it can only be concluded that the only path to spiritual, emotional, psychological, or physical healing; is one of the greatest scandals in all of humanity, forgiveness.

As far as the east is from the west, so far has he removed our transgressions from us (Psalm 103:12, NIV).

Personal Reflection

Probably a month or so after we had been living here at our new home in Norway, I completely broke down to my wife. I told her that I do not think I will ever get passed everything that we experienced in what we felt was a season of life that we were left completely shattered. I think it is a little more personal for me because of the location that we happened to be at during that season, and also possibly what God was teaching me that I needed to let go of. It was a place that is very close to my heart, it was home. I've referenced the *Voice of God* (Dante Bowe) quite a lot throughout this book. I suppose it's because it's a song we listened to and reflected on a lot during that shattered season of life. To keep my heart in the right place, and guard against only holding the memory of that challenging season on the days that I am thinking about and missing home, I try to personalize the message behind this great song and consider all of the ways in which God spoke to me there throughout my lifetime.

God spoke loudly through the cheers at my recreational softball games. I can reflect on how the sense of God's presence was with me in the fellowship around mom's chicken barbeque pit. Had I been listening for it, I may have heard His voice in the loud bursts of our shotguns shooting clay pigeons on Thanksgiving mornings. I can now see how his presence was even felt in fire hydrant sprinklers on back ally streets. Or even how I heard Him in the horse and buggy's coming down the country roads. Yes, I can even reflect on my high school years when I lived for playing Friday night football games. God's voice and presence was even there with me as I found joy in looking up in the stands and seeing family and hearing my name and number introduced through the loudspeaker.

I am forever grateful that amongst that hard season of life that God allowed me to go through by means of discerning what it truly means to give him all of me, that He was gracious in giving me the life that he did and now the spiritual lens to see and hear him in every aspect of my life from then until now. I am also thankful that while seasons change, his faithfulness and love endure and that he is always making things new. These days I am learning to listen for and discern the Spirit of God in new ways.

Living in a city that gets rainfall on average of 239 days a year, I choose to listen for His Spirit in the summer night Bergen rainfall. Our city is also surrounded by seven mountains, and so when we go on hikes to the top and I see the panoramic view, I have learned to embrace God's presence through the beauty of His creation. I sense God's spirit through the innocence of our kids jumping on the trampoline. I get just a minimal glimpse of the culture of

God's Heavenly Kingdom in hearing the three different languages (Norwegian, Spanish, English) spoken at our family gatherings. The fun weekend cabin trips that we take allow me to feel the Spiritual fruit of joy. It is quite amazing how the presence of God and the ways in which He speaks is all around us if we just take the time to seek it out.

Well, maybe it is not all bad that our shattered season of life will always be a part of me. The more I think about it, I think that is kind of the point of our shattered season(s), they break us to the point that nothing will ever be the same again. Seriously, through it all, I have learned to hear and see God in ways that I never have before. This is why it is imperative as Christians that we hold tight in desperation to God during these times. If we do not, I can tell you for a fact considering the place that my heart was in during my time in the transition within transition, that you will commit spiritual suicide. Had the harmful and evil desires of my heart during my transition time within transition been there for the entirety of my trying season, I would have essentially handed my heart and soul over to the devil. This is why our prayer daily should be, *search me, God, and know my heart; test me and know my anxious thoughts. See if there is any offensive way in me and lead me in the way everlasting* (Psalm 139:23-24, NIV).

The heart is deceitful above all things and beyond cure. Who can understand it (Jeremiah 17:9, NIV)? Sure, our shattered season(s) may be rough due to a lot of people, but it just may have more to do with the desires of our hearts. But if we can train our hearts, *through the renewing of our minds* (Romans 12:2, NIV), *to keep in mind the concerns of God and not human concerns* (Matthew 16:23, NIV); only then will we be truly equipped to find *glory in our sufferings, because we know that suffering produces perseverance; perseverance, character; and character, hope. And hope does not put us to shame, because God's love has been poured out into our hearts through the Holy Spirit who has been given to us* (Romans 5:3-4, NIV).

God does have an incredibly unique plan for each and every one of our lives. And as I sit here now personally reflecting on my shattered season, I can tell you that you just have to trust God's process and timing. The other night as my wife and I were talking, I said to her in a questioning tone that surely God has a plan for all of this. I continued by expressing that considering the fact that I am now physically far away from home as well as the place that my heart was in when we relocated to her home country regarding discouragement, disappointment, and even unforgiveness; in my heart I feel like I lost everything. But then I remembered what I determined God was trying to show me all along, *those of you who do not give up everything you have cannot be my disciples* (Luke 14:33, NIV). Everything we have as it relates to matters of the heart, *the Lord does not look at the things people look at. People look at the outward appearance, but the Lord looks at the heart* (1 Samuel 16:7, NIV).

For the first time in my entire life my heart is finally in a place that God can do a real work in it because it has unintentionally, but by the goodness of God, been emptied of everything that the depths of its desires once were. The only thing that keeps my heart alive and beating now, are the new desires being birthed from the Holy

Spirit's comfort in its *poor and mourning* (Matthew 5:3-4, NIV) state. None of this would have taken place without having gone through that shattered season of life.

So, while it's hard to actually praise God in the storm, when we reflect back and see where God has brought us as a result of it, we can absolutely praise God for the shattered season(s) of our lives.

"I can't count the times I've called your name some broken night. And you showed up and patched me up like you do every time. I get amnesia, I forget that you keep coming around. Good God almighty...I keep praising your name at the top of my lungs. Tell me is he good? He is good! Tell me is he God? He is God! He is good God almighty" (David Crowder, Good God Almighty)!

God's Plan

"The farmer was good, and the farmer was kind, and the farmer was always watching over them. Even when they didn't know it" (Lysa Terkeurst, It Will be Okay). I read this book a lot to my kids during the season of life that we felt shattered. I am pretty sure it comforted me a lot more than it did them though. I have yet to know what my God given assignment is on this earth, maybe it is no more than striving to be a faithful husband and father while taking the experiences of my shattered season(s) and teaching my children and others the importance of holding tight to God no matter what, during these times. In this children's book there was another line that I really held onto during this season of life. The book uses the analogy of a farmer planting a seed deep down in the dark and messy dirt so that it can grow at harvest. The seed's friend was looking for it one day and the seed responded, "I am here, I am here, way down in the dirt. I am scared and I am lonely, but I am not hurt" (Lysa Terkuerst, It Will Be Okay).

Maybe you have finally gotten to the end of this book, and while everything in these last few chapters seem hopeful, you are still planted deep down in a dark, lonely, and scary place. God is with you and I can assure you that he is watching over you! Maintain love in your heart for God *because all things work together for the good of those who love him, who have been called according to his purpose* (Romans 8:28, NIV). You have been called according to God's purpose, and *"what no eye has seen, what no ear has heard, and what no human mind has conceived" – the things that God has prepared for those who love him* (1 Corinthians 2:9, NIV).

"For I know the plans I have for you", declares the Lord, *"plans to prosper you and not to harm you, plans to give you hope and a future"* (Jeremiah 29:11, NIV). We can't even begin to fathom the mysteries and plans of God, that's why it says, "for I know the plans I have", nothing in there about you or me knowing and having our own plans. God's plan and will for our life is *good, pleasing, and perfect* (Romans 12:2, NIV), so hold tight to him and keep trusting him in the shattered season(s) of your life, I promise you that he will see you through!

Therefore, while the circumstances of each of our shattered season(s) are all different, the sting of the pain that results from them are all the same. So, let's reminisce on these song lyrics as a prophetic hope of the eternal outcome of our shattered season(s) of life.

I've lived stories that have proved your faithfulness. I've seen miracles my mind can't comprehend. There is beauty in what I cannot understand, Jesus it's you, Jesus it's you. I believe you're the wonder working God, you're the wonder working God, all the miracles I've seen, you're too good to not believe (Brandon Lake; Cody Carnes, Too Good to Not Believe).

God can do it for you! God will do it for you! Just hold on, he is carrying you through!